John D
Johnso
Johnson, VT. 05656

1974

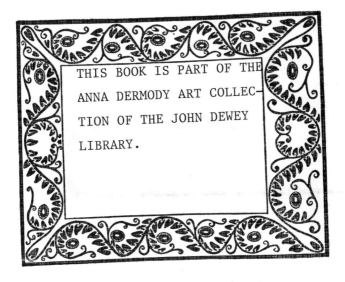

THIS BOOK IS PART OF THE ANNA DERMODY ART COLLECTION OF THE JOHN DEWEY LIBRARY.

The New Century Handbook of

GREEK ART AND ARCHITECTURE

The New Century Handbook of

GREEK ART AND ARCHITECTURE

edited by

Catherine B. Avery

APPLETON-CENTURY-CROFTS
Educational Division
MEREDITH CORPORATION
NEW YORK

R
709.38
N432
72 - 15071

Copyright © 1972 by
MEREDITH CORPORATION

All rights reserved. This book, or parts
thereof, must not be used or reproduced in
any manner without written permission. For
information address the publisher, Appleton-
Century-Crofts, Educational Division,
Meredith Corporation, 440 Park Avenue
South, New York, New York 10016

Selected from *The New Century Classical Handbook,*
edited by Catherine B. Avery
Copyright © 1962 by
APPLETON-CENTURY-CROFTS, INC.

72   73   74   75   76/10   9   8   7   6   5   4   3   2   1

Library of Congress Catalog Card Number:
72-187738

PRINTED IN THE UNITED STATES OF AMERICA

(R) 390-66942-3

Preface

Little remains intact of the wondrous works of beauty with which the Greeks ornamented their temples and shrines. The buildings are the victims of time, nature, and man. The free-standing sculptures and those of friezes, pediments, and metopes have too often been damaged by the same forces. Yet what remains is of such perfection and purity as to seem an ideal of artistic expression for all time. The Parthenon, the Temple of Apollo Epicurius at Bassae, the Theseum, maimed as they are, present an ardent beauty. *The Victory of Paeonius,* its fragments joined together by wires, still soars triumphant; unsurpassed still is the grace of *Nike Loosing Her Sandal.* Many more examples could be cited. Greek panel painting has almost entirely disappeared. Parts of frescoes have been recovered at Cnossus and, more recently, some magnificent examples (illustrated in the following pages) have been uncovered on the island of Thera, painstakingly removed and restored, and are now in the National Archaeological Museum, Athens. Other examples of Greek painting are to be found on the splendidly decorated pots of various sizes and for various uses that have been found in many parts of Greece and in other areas of the Greek world. The subjects on the panels of Greek vase-painting vary from mythology to matters of interest in everyday life.

THE NEW CENTURY HANDBOOK OF GREEK ART AND ARCHITECTURE presents in one alphabetical listing information on Greek sculpture and architects, painters and potters, temples and shrines. The text is enhanced with illustrations, and a 32-page insert of photographs offers a sampling of the development of the arts of sculpture and vase-painting over a period of centuries. Most of the articles have been drawn from THE NEW CENTURY CLASSICAL HANDBOOK, published by Appleton-Century-Crofts in 1962. New material has been added to a number of articles to take account of more recent archaeological finds, as those at Akrotiri on Thera, at the Piraeus, and elsewhere. Articles signed by the initials JJ were prepared by the late Jotham Johnson, Head of the Department of Classics, New York University, who served as Editorial Consultant for THE NEW CENTURY CLASSICAL HANDBOOK.

In offering THE NEW CENTURY HANDBOOK OF GREEK ART AND ARCHITECTURE, with its augmented text and additional illustrations, the publisher presents an introduction to a rare period in western art.

Catherine B. Avery

List of Photographs following page 86

List of Photographs

Sculptured base of column from the later temple of Artemis at Ephesus, marble, c340 B.C. *British Museum.*

Bronze statuette. Beroea, c400 B.C. *Antikensammlungen, Munich.*

Standing Woman. Terra-cotta figurine, 4th century B.C. *The Metropolitan Museum of Art (Rogers Fund, 1906).*

Head of a Young Goddess. Chios, marble, c300 B.C. *Courtesy of the Museum of Fine Arts, Boston. Gift of Nathaniel Thayer.*

Aphrodite. Terra-cotta statuette, end of 2nd century B.C. *Staatliche Museen, Berlin.*

Attic Geometric amphora, mid-8th century B.C. *Museum Antiker Kleinkunst, Munich. Hirmer Fotoarchiv München.*

Protoattic amphora, 7th century B.C. *Louvre. Hirmer Fotoarchiv München.*

Neck amphora, 7th century B.C. Neck: Heracles Slaying Nessus; body: Gorgons. *National Museum, Athens. T.A.P. Service.*

Corinthian wine-jug, 625–600 B.C. *British Museum.*

Early Corinthian alabastron, 625–600 B.C. *Louvre. Hirmer Fotoarchiv München.*

Middle Corinthian aryballus, early 6th century B.C. Griffin. *Staatliche Museen, Berlin. Hirmer Fotoarchiv München.*

Corinthian crater, end of 7th century B.C. Heracles Feasting with Eurytus. *Louvre.*

Attic black-figured dinos, c600–590 B.C. Death of Medusa. *Louvre.*

Cleitias, François Vase, c570 B.C. Neck: Calydonian Boar Hunt; Funeral Games for Patroclus. Body: Wedding of Peleus and Thetis; Achilles Pursuing Troilus; Real and Fabulous Animals. Foot: Battle of Cranes and Pygmies. *Museo Archeologico, Florence. Hirmer Fotoarchiv München.*

Arcesilaus Painter. Laconian cup, c565–560 B.C. King Arcesilaus Supervising the Weighing of Silphion. *Bibliothèque Nationale. Paris. Hirmer Fotoarchiv München.*

Black-figured hydria, mid-6th century B.C. Hermes Stealing Apollo's Cattle. *Louvre.*

Chalcidian crater, 550–530 B.C. Two Youths Preparing To Go Riding. *British Museum.*

Chalcidian hydria, c550–530 B.C. Zeus Attacking Typhon. *Museum Antiker Kleinkunst, Munich.*

Amasis Painter. Neck amphora, c540 B.C. Dionysus and Maenads. *Bibliothèque Nationale, Paris. Hirmer Fotoarchiv München.*

Exekias. Cup interior, c535 B.C. Dionysus in a Boat. *Museum Antiker Kleinkunst, Munich. Hirmer Fotoarchiv München.*

Tleson Painter. Signed cup interior, 3rd quarter of 6th century B.C. Hunter. *British Museum.*

——A——

Abacus (ab'a̱-kus). In architecture, the slab or plinth which forms the upper member of the capital of a column or pillar, and upon which rests, in classic styles, the lower surface of the architrave. In the Greek Doric it is thick and square, without sculptured decoration; in the Ionic order it is thinner, and ornamented with moldings on the sides; in the Corinthian also it is ornamented, and has concave sides and truncated corners.

Acropolis (a̱-krop'ọ̄-lis). A general name for the citadel of an ancient Greek city. The name is especially appropriated to that of Athens, whose Acropolis is a precipitous rock that rises about 260 feet above the city, extends 1000 feet from E to W, and is 400 feet in its greatest width. It forms a natural citadel, and in earliest times was the site of ancient Athens itself, strongly fortified and containing the palace of the king. It was a center of worship from most ancient times. Here were the palaces of Cecrops and Erechtheus, and here Athena vied with Poseidon for control of the city.

The well of Clepsydra, below the northwest corner of the Acropolis and reached in ancient times by a covered stairway, supplied the citadel with water. Nearby was the cave where Apollo is said to have ravished Creusa, daughter of Erechtheus, and fathered Ion, ancestor of the Ionians. Traces of settlements of the Neolithic Age have been found on the slopes of the

---

fat, fāte, fär, fâll, a̱sk, fãre; net, mē, hėr; pin, pīne; not, nōte, möve, nôr; up, lūte, půll; oi, oil; ou out; (lightened) ẹlect, agọ̄ny, ūnite; (obscured) errạnt, ardẹnt, actọr; ch, chip; g, go; th, thin; ŦH, then; y, you; (variable) d̪ as d or j, s̪ as s or sh, t̪ as t or ch, z̪ as z or zh.

1

Acropolis. The first palace on its upper surface was erected between 1900 and 1600 B.C. Traces of structures of the age of Cecrops (traditional date, 1581 B.C.), Erechtheus, and other early kings include a palace, parts of Pelasgian walls, and the platform where the temple of Nike stands. Traces of a temple from the period 1100–750 B.C. also survive. Down to about the 7th century B.C. the Acropolis was a fortified citadel. After that time it came to be considered as a sacred area and private dwellings were removed from it, leaving a few temples and a simple propylaeum. The foundations of an ancient temple of Athena, lying between and partly under the sites where the *Erechtheum* and the *Parthenon* now stand, were recognized and studied by Dörpfeld in 1885. The Doric, peripteral temple, which measured 70 by 137 feet, went through three phases. The earliest part of it was raised on the foundations of a prehistoric Mycenaean palace about the time of Solon (c638–c559 B.C.), and was entirely dedicated to Athena Polias. Toward the end of the 6th century B.C. the Pisistratidae, seeking to equal the beautiful temple erected by their rivals the Alcmaeonidae at Delphi, transformed the naos of the temple and, 520–510 B.C., added 12 columns on the flanks, six columns on the façades, and painted marble pediments. The temple was destroyed by the Persians, 480 B.C., and was partly restored. In 454 B.C. the treasury of the Confederacy of Delos was brought from Delos and placed in the restored temple. On completion of the Parthenon the treasury was removed thither. After the completion of the Erechtheum (407 B.C.), the restored section of the ancient temple of Athena Polias fell into disuse. It was destroyed by fire in 406 B.C. and its foundations were covered over by a terrace. In the 6th century B.C. there was a temple on the present site of the Parthenon, and many smaller temples and treasuries as well on the Acropolis. In this century Pisistratus and Clisthenes made additions to the temples. All of these were com-

fat, fāte, fär, fåll, åsk, fãre; net, mē, hèr; pin, pīne; not, nōte, möve, nôr; up, lūte, půll; oi, oil; ou out; (lightened) ĕlect, agǫny, ūnite;

pletely destroyed when the Persians attacked, took the citadel and burned it, 480 B.C. After the successes of the Greeks at Salamis (480) and Plataea (479 B.C.), the Athenians returned to the city which they had abandoned when the Persians swept down on it. Themistocles, the successful commander at Salamis and the most influential man in Athens, immediately set about rebuilding the walls of the city and those on the north side of the Acropolis as well, using drums of the columns of the ancient temple of Athena and other marble fragments created by the Persian destruction as building materials. These fragments, set into the wall in a kind of pattern and plainly visible to all, were a constant reminder to the Athenians of the Persian vandalism. Cimon continued the work of Themistocles. He built walls on the east and south slopes and increased the top area by filling it in with the rubble that was strewn about the Acropolis. By the time of Pericles (c495–429 B.C.), the Acropolis had been shored up by walls and its area increased but its surface was a mass of ruins. Cleared of ancient structures of varying periods, it presented a site for a planned development of new buildings. Pericles seized this opportunity to create here a great religious center and artistic memorial to the victory of the Greeks over the Persians. Ictinus, Callicrates, and Phidias were given the responsibility and authority to carry out his plan. The buildings and remains from this period (last half of the 5th century B.C.) make of the Acropolis a world-famous monument of the Classical period. The traveler Pausanias describes the Acropolis as it was in the 2nd century A.D. His description, the only complete contemporary account of any age, provides a full description of buildings, statues, and altars that have since disappeared, and also makes possible the identification of many objects that have remained.

In the Pelasgic period (1600–1100 B.C.) the Acropolis could be approached by a stairway cut into rock at

(obscured) errạnt, ardẹnt, actọr; ch, chip; g, go; th, thin; ŦH, then; y, you; (variable) ḍ as d or j, ş as s or sh, ţ as t or ch, ẓ as z or zh.

the northeast corner. This led to the palace of the ancient kings. The natural entrance was on the west, through the *Enneapylon,* the nine gates that were added to the Acropolis perhaps in the 10th century B.C. By the time of Pausanias the main entrance was by a great gate, the *Propylaea* on the west. This vast, never-completed structure was designed by Mnesicles. His design, majestic and symmetrical, had to be altered when

Propylaea and Temple of Athena Nike

priests of Athena Nike and Brauronian Artemis refused to allow their ancient precincts to be invaded to make room for the south side of the proposed Propylaea. Work on the structure was begun in 438 B.C., but was halted 431 B.C. by the outbreak of the

fat, fāte, fär, fâll, ȧsk, fãre; net, mē, hėr; pin, pīne; not, nōte, mȯve, nôr; up, lūte, pu̇ll; oi, oil; ou out; (lightened) ēlect, agǫny, ūnite;

Peloponnesian Wars. The design was modified in succeeding centuries and additions were made to it. Among the last of these was that by Caligula in 40 A.D. The present approach to the Propylaea is by the *Beulé Gate,* so-called because it was uncovered by the French archaeologist Ernest Beulé in 1853. A western extension of the Propylaea, it was added perhaps in the 2nd century A.D., and was covered by the Turks when they used the Acropolis as a fortress. The Propylaea were transformed into an archbishop's palace (12th century), and were later used for administrative offices; about the middle of the 17th century the Turks who had occupied the Acropolis since 1394 stored gunpowder there. This was ignited by a thunderbolt and exploded. Thus, part of the structure was destroyed (1640). It is now being restored. In ancient times a winding path was followed by the sacred processions to the Acropolis in the Panathenaic festival. This was replaced by a marble ramp that led to the Propylaea. On the south or right side of the Propylaea is the little temple of Athena Nike, goddess of Victory, built on a bastion that juts out to the west, on a site that was from ancient times a precinct of Athena. The ancient cult image was of wood, and depicted the goddess without wings, holding in one hand a pomegranate, symbol of peace and fertility, and in the other her war helmet. This edifice came to be known as the temple of *Nike Apteros* (Wingless Victory) perhaps from the ancient statue. Here, some say, Victory was presented as wingless so that she could never fly from Athens. The exquisite relief sculptures of the Victories, including the charming *Victory Loosing Her Sandal,* from the balustrade of the temple, are now in the museum on the Acropolis. On the site of the temple of Athena Nike, so legend says, Aegeus stood to look over the sea, watching for the ship whose sails would tell him the fate of Theseus. From here, when he saw the black sails of death, he hurled himself to the rocks below. The temple of Athena Nike, built 440 B.C., was pulled down by the Turks in 1687, and its material was used by them to build a rampart against the Venetians. It was carefully reconstructed from its original pieces in 1835, later found to be near a state of collapse, and in 1936–41 was rebuilt again, when remains of an older temple were found. To the left of the Propylaea was what Pausanias referred to as a building with pictures, the *Pinacotheca*. Among the pictures he mentions in it were representations of Diomedes taking the Palladium from Troy, Odysseus fetching Philoctetes at Lemnos, Orestes killing Aegisthus, Pylades killing the sons of Nauplius who had come to the aid of Aegisthus, and Polyxena about to be sacrificed on the tomb of Achilles. There were many more pictures, but all of these and the foregoing have been lost. Inside the Propylaea, at the entrance to the Acropolis, was a figure of *Hermes of the Gateway*. Near it was a small stone on which Silenus was supposed to have sat and rested when he came in the train of Dionysus to Athens.

To the south center of the Acropolis is the Parthenon, a temple that for strength and simplicity, perfect proportions and harmonious relation to its site, has never been equalled. This was Athena's great temple, named from her epithet Athena Parthenos. Pericles engaged Ictinus as architect and gave Phidias general charge of its construction and ornamentation. Periods in history when such a fortunate combination of geniuses lived at the same time have been rare. Work on the temple, which faces the east, was commenced in 447 and completed in 438 B.C. On its pediments were great sculptured scenes, skillfully designed to fit the awkward and constricted area of a thin elongated triangle with perfect grace. The scene at the birth of Athena was on the east pediment; the west pediment showed the contest of Athena and Poseidon. The building was richly decorated inside and out. Great artists worked on it; rich gifts were made to it in succeeding times,

7

The Acropolis, with Erechtheum and Parthenon, from the south
Greek National Tourist Office

(obscured) errant, ardent, actor; ch, chip; g, go; th, thin; ᵮH, then; y, you;
(variable) ḏ as d or j, ş as s or sh, ţ as t or ch, ẕ as z or zh.

among them the golden shields presented by Alexander the Great after the battle of the Granicus, 334 B.C. In later times, when Christianity spread over the Mediterranean world and the Emperor Theodosius II destroyed many of the great monuments, the Parthenon was dedicated as a Christian church (630 A.D.). Later it was turned into a mosque and equipped with minarets by the Turks, who had occupied the Acropolis since 1394, and it was used by them as an arsenal in a war with the Venetians. During the siege a shot from the Hill of the Muses pierced the roof, ignited the gunpowder stored there, and blew the magnificent building apart (1687). This was the worst disaster that had ever befallen it. Afterward its monumental sculptures, statues, altars, and columns lay in broken heaps on the ground. In succeeding years some of the marble was carried away and used for building material. Early in the 19th century Lord Elgin, ambassador of Great Britain in Constantinople, received permission from the Sultan to gather up what he wished of the fallen and neglected marbles and to carry them off to England, where they were placed in the British Museum, 1816. (The so-called Elgin Marbles, exhibited in the British Museum, are in incomparably better condition than the friezes and fragments that have remained exposed on the Acropolis. Now, the worst enemy of the marbles, including the structures, still on the Acropolis is air pollution.) Across from the Parthenon, to the north, rises the Erechtheum, built after 421 B.C., on the site of one of the oldest sanctuaries of the Acropolis. Here, according to tradition, Athena and Poseidon vied for control of Athens. Poseidon struck the rock with his trident, and a fountain of sea water gushed forth. Athena gave the olive tree as her gift to the city. It was voted the more useful to man and she was awarded the city and became its chief goddess. The Erechtheum housed the ancient shrines of the rivals. The cella in the east of the building was that of Athena.

fat, fāte, fär, fâll, ȧsk, fāre; net, mē, hėr; pin, pīne; not, nōte, möve, nôr; up, lūte, pu̇ll; oi, oil; ou out; (lightened) ĕlect, agǫny, ūnite;

In it was the ancient olive-wood image of the goddess, said to have fallen from heaven in the time of Cecrops. It was burned when the Persians destroyed the Acropolis, or, as some say, was saved by being taken aboard a Greek ship just before the battle of Salamis (480 B.C.). Behind the cella of Athena, to the west, was the cella of Poseidon-Erechtheus. Thus the two rival immortals, Athena and Poseidon, were united in one temple. In Poseidon's cella was enclosed the fountain of sea water, sometimes called the "Sea of Erechtheus," brought forth by Poseidon's trident, as well as the marks of his trident. It was said that when the south wind blew the cistern gave forth the sound of waves. There were also altars to Hephaestus, a god closely associated with Athena in the arts of civilization, and to Butes, an ancient priest of Athena and ancestor of the priestly family, the Butadae. Behind the cella of Poseidon was the *Pandroseum,* the sanctuary of Pandrosos, daughter of Cecrops and first priestess of Athena. In the enclosure was the sacred olive tree Athena planted as a gift to Athens. The tree was burned during the Persian Wars, but according to tradition it immediately put forth a new shoot. The famous *Porch of the Maidens* formed a south wing of the Erechtheum, and a north porch was a place of sacrifices to Zeus. The Erechtheum was converted into a church, probably in the 7th century A.D., and in the time of the Turkish occupation it housed the harem of the Turkish commander on the Acropolis. Many altars and statues were on the Acropolis, among them the statue of *Athena Lemnia* by Phidias, said by Pausanias to be his finest work. There were also numberless statues representing scenes from mythology, images of the gods, and of such mortals as Pericles, Xanthippus, and Anacreon of Teos, the poet. On the south slope of the Acropolis was the sanctuary of Asclepius, begun c420 B.C., an important healing center until its close in the 5th century A.D. To the east of the sanctuary of As-

(obscured) errạnt, ardẹnt, actọr; ch, chip; g, go; th, thin; ᴛʜ, then; y, you; (variable) ḍ as d or j, ṣ as s or sh, ṭ as t or ch, ẓ as z or zh.

clepius are the remains of a theater of Dionysus built in the 4th century B.C. on the site of the ancient theater in which the plays of Aeschylus, Sophocles, and Euripides had been performed. At the southeast corner on the lower slopes was the *Odeum,* constructed about the same time as the Parthenon.

In 86 B.C. Sulla besieged Athens and destroyed many buildings on the south slope of the Acropolis. In Roman times additions were made to the Propylaea and buildings were added on the Acropolis. A circular shrine dedicated to the goddess Roma and to the Emperor Augustus was erected 14 B.C. Hadrian made rich gifts and repaired buildings. Herodes Atticus, wealthy Athenian and generous donor of buildings, built the theater named for him on the south slope, in memory of his wife Regilla, c160 A.D. From the reign of Theodosius II (401–450 A.D.), the Acropolis ceased to be a center of worship. He caused the monuments to be mutilated or destroyed in a ruthless campaign of Christianization. As noted earlier, the Acropolis was occupied by the Turks for about 400 years. In 1833, following the liberation of the Greeks, the royal ensign of their first king, Otto I, was hoisted on the Acropolis. Almost immediately work was begun on the restoration of the monuments, among the most precious in the western world. Excavations have revealed successively earlier stages of development, before the time of Pericles. The site, crowned by the Parthenon, the Erechtheum whose more delicate outlines, façade, and famous Porch of the Maidens are in good state of preservation, and the temple of Athena Nike, is a center of artistic and cultural pilgrimage. Large marble fragments and the drums of columns of these and other structures remain where they fell, in the hope that means will be found to reassemble and raise them.

Acroterium (ak-rọ-tē′ri-um). A small pedestal placed on the apex or angle of a pediment for the support of a statue or other ornament; the statue or ornament

fat, fāte, fär, fȧll, ȧsk, fãre; net, mē, hėr; pin, pīne; not, nōte, möve, nôr; up, lūte, pṳll; oi, oil; ou out; (lightened) ẹlect, agọny, ṵnite;

placed on such a pedestal; also, any ornament forming the apex of a building or of a monument. Acroteria were frequently employed in the ornamentation of Greek temples and monuments.

Adytum (ad'i-tum). In ancient worship, a sacred place which the worshipers might not enter, or which might be entered only by those who had performed certain rites, or only by males or by females, or only on certain appointed days, etc. Also, a secret sanctuary or shrine open only to the priests, or whence oracles were delivered, hence in general the most sacred or reserved part of any place of worship. In Greece an adytum was usually an inner recess or chamber in a temple as in that of Hera at Aegium; but it might be an entire temple as that of Poseidon at Mantinea, or a grove, inclosure, or cavern, as the sacred inclosure of Zeus on the Lycaean mount in Arcadia. The most famous adytum of Greece was the sanctuary of the Pythic oracle at Delphi.

Head of Athena,
from the E pediment
of the so-called Temple of
Aphaea, Aegina, c490 B.C.
Glyptothek, Munich

Aeginetan Marbles (ej-i-nē'tạn). Pediment sculptures and acroteria from the temple of Aphaea on the Greek island of Aegina, found in 1811 and now in the Glyptothek, Munich. Study of them is complicated by the fact that three sets of pediment sculptures survive, suggesting that perhaps one of the original sets was damaged

Heracles, from the E pediment of the so-called Temple of Aphaea, Aegina, c490 B.C.
Glyptothek, Munich

and replaced. They were restored by the sculptor Thorwaldsen, who sawed off the broken stumps of limbs the more neatly to attach his restorations, with the result that when 20th-century excavators found additional fragments it proved impossible to refer

fat, fāte, fär, fåll, åsk, fãre; net, mē, hèr; pin, pīne; not, nōte, möve, nôr; up, lūte, pụll; oi, oil; ou out; (lightened) ẹlect, agǫny, ụnite;

them to their original positions. All three pediments show scenes of combat between Greeks and Trojans. They date from c510 B.C. and the period of 490–480 B.C. (JJ)

Temple of Aphaea, Aegina, 6th century B.C.

Aeschines (es'ki-nēz) *the Orator.* Greek statue from Herculaneum, in the National Museum at Naples, of high rank among works of its class. The orator stands quietly, his arm wrapped in his mantle; the expression is preoccupied but full of dignity.

Aëtion (ā-ē'shi-ọn). Greek painter, mid-4th century B.C., probably a contemporary of Apelles. He is noted for his painting *The Marriage of Alexander and Roxana.*

Agasias (ạ-gā'shi-as). Name of two Greek sculptors of the Ephesian school who lived sometime during the 1st century B.C.: 1) Son of Dositheus. His name is inscribed on the base of the *Borghese Gladiator* in the Louvre in Paris. 2) Son of Menophilus. A military statue done by him is in the Athens national museum.

Agatharchus (ag-a-thär′kus). Athenian painter; born on the island of Samos in the Aegean Sea; fl. c460–417 B.C. He is said by Vitruvius to have painted a scene for a tragedy by Aeschylus, and thus is sometimes credited with having been the inventor of scene-painting for the theater.

Ageladas (aj-e-lā′das). [Also: *Hageladas, Hagelaidas.*] Greek sculptor, a native of Argos; fl. c520–c460 B.C. He was noted for his statues of gods and athletes in bronze, of which no originals now exist, and is thought to have been the instructor of Myron, Phidias, and Polyclitus.

Agesander (aj-e-san′dèr) or *Agesandros* (-dros). Greek sculptor, a native of Rhodes, active 42–21 B.C. With Athenodorus and Polydorus of Rhodes he carved the famous sculptured group known as the *Laocoön*. This depicts the episode narrated by Aeneas in the second book of Vergil's *Aeneid,* when, following the priest Laocoön's bidding the Trojans to trust not the Wooden Horse ("I fear the Greeks even bearing gifts"), two great serpents emerge from the sea and attack Laocoön and his two sons. A copy of this sculpture (or possibly the original), is in the Vatican Museum, Rome. Fragments of sculpture recently found in a cave of Sperlonga, Italy, were at first assigned to a second Laocoön group, but some scholars prefer another interpretation. (JJ)

Agora (ag′o-ra). The Greek term meaning "market-place," analogous to the forums of Roman cities. Essentially, it is a considerable open space within the walls; the political, social, and commercial focus of the community where farmers bring their produce for retail sale, businessmen meet their clients and associates, and popular assemblies may be convoked. It is often bordered by stoas (colonnades, porticoes), public offices, and a temple or two. One who speaks of "the Agora," without specifying which city's agora he

---

fat, fāte, fär, fȧll, ȧsk, fāre; net, mē, hèr; pin, pīne; not, nōte, möve, nôr; up, lūte, pùll; oi, oil; ou out; (lightened) ēlect, agǫny, ūnite;

means, presumably refers to that of Athens, most famous for its association with the city's intellectual and artistic, as well as political and economic, leadership of classical Greece. The Athenian Agora is a broad area extending from the northwest slopes of the Acropolis to the terrace on which the Temple of Hephaestus stands, revealed by extensive excavations conducted by an American mission from 1931 to the present. (JJ)

Agoracritus (ag-ọ-rak′ri-tus) or *Agorakritos* (-tos). Greek sculptor, born on the island of Paros in the Aegean Sea, and active in the 5th century B.C. He was a favorite pupil of Phidias and a rival of Alcamenes. He is now remembered chiefly for his work on the *Nemesis at Rhamnus,* fragments of which are in the British Museum and the National Museum, Athens. But some say this statue was by Phidias himself. The bronze image of *Athena Itonia* in the temple at Boeotia was made by Agoracritus.

Akrotiri (ak-rọ-tē′ri). Town on the southern coast of Thera (Santorini), near the site of a Minoan outpost buried by a volcanic eruption possibly about 1500 B.C. Excavations, begun with the discovery of the ancient city in 1967, have uncovered streets and buildings yielding a number of valuable finds. The most remarkable of these are the frescoes, which are to be housed in the National Museum at Athens. "The Room of the Lilies," covering 140 square feet, is the largest nearly intact fresco of that period ever found in Greece. Covering three walls of a room, it depicts red lilies growing from multicolored volcanic rocks as swallows hover around. Several other frescoes, found in fragments and now partially restored, depict such scenes as blue monkeys playing on red lava rocks ("The Monkeys"), two boys boxing ("Fresco of the Princes"), and two stylized antelopes. Fragments of other frescoes show a young priestess making an offering, a woman picking flowers, and stylized flower motifs. Among the other finds are household utensils, bronze vessels, and pot-

(obscured) errạnt, ardẹnt, actọr; ch, chip; g, go; th, thin; ₮H, then; y, you; (variable) ḍ as d or j, ṣ as s or sh, ṭ as t or ch, ẓ as z or zh.

tery decorated with floral and spiral designs or stylized
birds and other animal designs.

FRESCO OF THE PRINCES
Detail, Young Prince, Akrotiri, Thera
National Museum, Athens
T.A.P. Service

TWO ANTELOPES
Fresco found at Akrotiri, Thera; Fresco of the Princes on side wall
National Museum, Athens
T.A.P. Service

(obscured) errạnt, ardẹnt, actọr; ch, chip; g, go; th, thin; ͏H, then; y, you;
(variable) ḍ as d or j, ṣ as s or sh, ţ as t or ch, ẓ as z or zh.

Alabastrum (al-a-bas'trum) or *Alabastron* (-tron). In ancient Greece, a small elongated vase for unguents or
perfumes, rounded at the bottom and provided with a
broad rim about a small orifice. Vases of this class were
originally so called because they were made of alabas-
ter; but the name was applied also to vessels of similar
form and use in other materials, as metal, glass (sometimes richly ornamented in color), or pottery.

Alcamenes or *Alkamenes* (al-kam'e-nēz). Greek sculptor,
born at Lemnos or Athens and active c450–c400 B.C.
According to Pausanias he was the most skillful pupil
of Phidias and, like him, worked in gold, ivory, and
bronze as well as in marble. He probably assisted
Phidias in the decoration of the Parthenon. He is
known to have done *Aphrodite of the Gardens* (a copy of
which is now at Athens), which is considered a masterpiece of his period, and bronze cult statues of Athena
and Hephaestus in the temple of Hephaestus over-
looking the Athenian Agora. The famous caryatids of
the Maiden Porch of the Erechtheum on the Athenian
Acropolis have also been attributed to him, on stylistic
grounds.

Alkamenes (al-kam'e-nēz). See *Alcamenes.*

Altis (al'tis). The sacred precinct of Zeus at Olympia.
About the sacred grove rose the installations connected with the Olympic Games, including the temples
of Zeus and Hera, treasuries, administrative buildings,
and the stadium.

Amasis (a-mā'sis). Attic potter of the 6th century B.C.
Eight vessels signed "Amasis made me" are extant.
They date from c555–525 B.C. The decorator of his
vessels worked in the black-figure style and is called
the Amasis Painter. Among his extant works an amphora (Paris) shows Dionysus holding a cantharus.
Two maenads, an arm of each about the other's neck,
approach to offer him small animals. An amphora
(Metropolitan Museum, New York), c550 B.C. attributed to the Amasis Painter, shows warriors departing for battle.

Library
Johnson State College
Johnson VT 05656

Amazonomachia (am″a̱-zon-ō̱-mak′i-a̱). In Greek antiquity, a battle of Amazons. There were several of these mythical battles: 1) the invasion of Lycia by the Amazons; 2) the invasion of Phrygia by the Amazons; 3) the battle with Heracles, his ninth labor, in which Hippolyte, queen of the Amazons, was slain; 4) the battle with Theseus to liberate Antiope; 5) the battle at the close of the Trojan War when the Amazons came to the assistance of Priam; 6) the Amazons' invasion of the island of Leuce at the mouth of the Ister. Since it furnished many interesting arrangements of men, women, and horses in action, the Amazonomachia was a favorite subject with Greek artists. One of the finest representations is a series of bas-reliefs in the British Museum which was found in the ruins of the Mausoleum at Halicarnassus.

Amphiareum (am″fi-ar′e̱-um). Sanctuary and oracle of Amphiaraus, near Oropus, in Boeotia, Greece. In Greek legend, Amphiaraus was one of the Seven who marched against Thebes, and was here swallowed up by the earth at the will of Zeus, to save him in his flight. The sanctuary occupies a narrow area on the bank of a torrent; it includes a temple and altar, a large portico, a long range of bases for votive statues, and a theater. All the existing ruins are of Hellenistic date. The oracle enjoyed great renown, and the deified seer had a high reputation for healing sickness. Excavations were made (1884 *et seq.*) here by the Archaeological Society of Athens.

Amphiprostylus (am-fi-prō̱-stī′lus). A Greek or Roman rectangular temple with a portico at both front and rear, but no columns on the flanks.

Amphora (am′fō̱-ra̱). A tall, slender vessel, having two handles or ears, a narrow neck, and generally a sharp-pointed base for insertion into a stand or into the ground: used by the Greeks and Romans for transporting and storing wine, oil, honey, grain, etc. They were commonly made of hard-baked, unglazed clay, but Homer mentions amphorae of gold. Amphorae with painted decoration, having lids and provided with bases enabling them to stand independently, served commonly as ornaments among the Greeks and were

AMPHORA
Athlete Carrying a Tripod, c540 B.C.
The Metropolitan Museum of Art

given as prizes in racing and athletic contests. The Panathenaic amphorae were large vases of this class, bearing designs relating to the worship of Athena. Filled with oil from the sacred olives, they were given at Athens as prizes to the victors in the Panathenaic games.

Andocides (an-dos′i-dēz). Attic potter, active at the end of the 6th century B.C. Seven vessels signed by him as potter are extant. Four of these were decorated by the same painter, who for this reason and because his own name is not known, is known as the Andocides Painter. Twenty-six other works have been attributed to the Andocides Painter. He was one of the first and most important of the vase painters to use the red-figure technique. He also used the black-figure style to decorate the craters and cups he painted. An amphora (Munich) has on one side Heracles feasting, attended by Athena, Hermes and a cupbearer, in the black-figure style. On the other side Heracles feasting, attended by Athena, appears in the red-figure style (c510 B.C.). Works signed by Andocides as potter and decorated by the Andocides Painter include: an amphora (Louvre) with a man playing the cithara, and a combat; an amphora (Louvre) with women bathing; a kylix (Palermo) with archers and a trumpeter; and an amphora (Berlin)

ANDOCIDES PAINTER
Heracles Feasting, red-figured amphora, c510 B.C.
Munich

with Heracles and Apollo struggling for the Delphic tripod. Other works include an amphora (Boston) c520 B.C., with Heracles driving a bull, and an amphora (Louvre) with Heracles dragging Cerberus from Hades.

Anta (an′tạ). In Greek and Roman architecture the pilaster that terminates one of the side walls of a building when these are prolonged beyond the face of the end wall. A portico *in antis* (that is, between antae) is formed when the side walls are thus prolonged and columns stand between the antae.

Antefix (an′tē-fiks). In classical architecture, an upright ornament, generally of marble or terra-cotta, placed at the eaves of a tiled roof, at the end of the last tile of each ridge of tiling, to conceal the joining of the tiles. Antefixes were also often placed at the junction of the tiles along the ridge of a roof, forming a cresting. In some Roman examples the antefixes were so disposed and combined with water channels as to serve as gargoyles.

Antenor (an-tē′nọr). Athenian sculptor of the 6th century B.C. He executed the first bronze statues of Harmodius and Aristogiton which the Athenians set up in the Agora and which were carried off to Susa by Xerxes I. After his conquest of Persia, Alexander the Great is said to have sent the statues back to Athens. A statue-base found on the Athenian Acropolis bears the signature of Antenor, and to this has been joined a marble *Kore,* also found on the Acropolis and plausibly ascribed to him.

Anthemion (an-thē′mi-ọn). In art and archaeology, a characteristic palmette or honeysuckle ornament, varying in detail but constant in type, of frequent occurrence both in single examples and in series, in vase-painting, in architectural sculpture, in jewelry and dress fabrics, and in all other decorative work of Greek origin from very early times, and later in ornament derived from the Greek. This ornament in its original shape was borrowed by Greek artists from the Orient, and was probably first adopted by the Ionians. It was much used upon antefixes, both sculptured and terra-cotta, and in the composition of acroteria, particularly those of the tall and slender Greek funeral slabs.

Anthemion frieze or molding. A molding or frieze ornamented with a series of anthemia, usually in graceful alternation of two forms. Sometimes the effect is diversified by the introduction of flowers or tendrils more literally expressed, and occasionally birds are represented perching on the tendrils, as in examples at Athens and Argos. The most elegant examples of anthemion molding are those beneath the capitals of the north porch columns, and forming one of the friezes, of the Erechtheum at Athens.

Antimachides (an-ti-mā′ki-dēz). Sixth century B.C. Greek architect associated with Antistates, Callaeschrus, and Porinus in preparing the original plans for the Olympieum, the colossal temple of Zeus Olympius at Athens projected by the Pisistratids. (JJ)

Antiphilus (an-tif′i-lus). Greek painter of the second half of the 4th century B.C. His work included portraits of Philip of Macedonia, Alexander the Great, and others.

Antistates (an-tis′ta̱-tēz). Greek architect, 6th century B. C., associated with Callaeschrus, Antimachides, and Porinus in preparing the original plans for the Olympieum, the colossal Doric dipteral temple of Zeus Olympius at Athens, construction of which was begun about 530 B.C. by the Pisistratids. Work on the temple was abandoned on the expulsion of Hippias, c510, resumed in 174 B.C. under the direction of the Roman architect Cossutius, and completed in the reign of the emperor Hadrian. (JJ)

Apelles (a̱-pel′ēz). Greek painter, born in Ionia, and active in the 4th century B.C. He is considered one of the great ancient artists. He is said to have been a pupil first of an otherwise unknown Ephorus of Ephesus, later of Pamphilus of Sicyon, and his style is described as a blend of Ionian and Dorian elements. He was celebrated particularly for his portraits, including one of Alexander the Great with the thunderbolts of Zeus, for the temple of Artemis at Ephesus, and those of such other Macedonian notables as Archelaus, Clitus, and Antigonus. He also painted a procession of the high priest of Artemis, Artemis and her nymphs, and the *Aphrodite Anadyomene* (Aphrodite wringing out her hair as she rises from the sea) painted for the temple of Asclepius at Cos. This last was probably his most noted work. It was taken to Rome by Augustus and set up in the temple of Caesar.

Apollino (ä-pōl-lē′nō). Statue in the collection of the Uffizi, Florence. It is an antique copy from a Greek original, probably of the 4th century B.C., representing a delicately built type of the youthful Apollo, standing easily and gracefully.

Apollo Belvedere (a̯-pol′ō; bel-ve̯-dir′; Italian, ä-pôl′lō bel-vä-dä′rä). Most famous extant statue of Apollo, a marble figure carved during the early Roman empire, now in the collection of the Belvedere, Vatican, Rome, discovered (1485) at Antium (now Anzio, Italy). It was copied from a Greek original in bronze. Just over life size, it depicts a vigorous, youthful god wearing a chlamys around the neck and over the extended left arm. The left hand, one of the parts restored by Montorsoli, a pupil of Michelangelo, holds part of an object variously thought to have been an aegis, a bow from which he has shot an arrow, or another weapon. The original may have been a commemorative figure erected at Delphi to celebrate the expulsion of the Gauls (279 B.C.) from the temple of Apollo.

Apollodorus (a-pol-o̯-dō′rus). [Surnamed *Sciagraphus,* meaning "Shadow Painter" or "Shadower."] Greek painter, contemporary of Zeuxis and Parrhasius. He was born at Athens and flourished in the late 5th century B.C. He seems to have been the first important painter to abandon the old schematic arrangements in painting in favor of shading by gradation of color and fore-shortening observed from nature.

Apollonius of Tralles (ap-o̯-lō′ni-us; tral′ēz). Greek sculptor, born at Tralles, in Caria, who was active probably in the 1st century B.C. With his brother Tauriscus he carved the so-called *Farnese Bull,* representing the death of Dirce.

Apollo Sauroktonos (a̯-pol′ō sô-rok′tō̯-nos). [Also: *Sauroc-*

tonus; Eng. trans., "the Lizard-slayer."] Name of two copies, one in bronze (Vatican, Rome) and one in marble (Paris), of a lost bronze statue by the Greek sculptor Praxiteles. The god leans against a tree and is apparently about to strike with an arrow, possibly as a method of divination, the lizard which climbs up the trunk. The relaxed, curving figure is typical of Praxiteles' choice of youthful subjects and his graceful, humanizing treatment of the gods.

Archelaus (är-kẹ-lā′us). Greek sculptor of the 1st century A.D. A bas-relief, the *Apotheosis of Homer,* carved by him, is in the British Museum.

Architrave (är′ki-trāv). In architecture, the member of an entablature that rests immediately on the column and supports those portions of the structure that are above it.

Argive Heraeum. A famous sanctuary of Hera, patron goddess of Argos, situated on a spur of Mount Euboea between Argos and Mycenae. It contains on three terraces the remains of a 6th-century Doric temple which was burned in 423 B.C., the late 5th-century Doric temple which replaced it, and a number of stoas or colonnades excavated in 1892–95 by the American School of Classical Studies at Athens under the direction of Charles Waldstein. The temple was notable for its cult statue in gold and ivory by Polyclitus. In legend, it was at this shrine that the Greek chieftains swore allegiance to Agamemnon before leaving for Troy, and Herodotus tells Solon's story of Cleobis and Biton, sons of a priestess of Hera, who, when the team assigned to draw their mother to the shrine failed to arrive, yoked themselves to the car and drew her to the Heraeum. After which, having sacrificed and feasted, they lay down, never to awake. (JJ)

Aristides of Thebes (ar-is-tī′dēz). [Also: *Aristeides.*] Greek painter; fl. 4th century B.C. He did battle scenes, hunting scenes, and other works, prized by Alexander and others for their expression of the mind and passions of man. His most famous painting represented a conquered city. In it a mother, dying, thrusts back the infant who seeks her breast, to prevent the child from sucking blood.

Aryballus (ar-i-bal′us). A form of Greek vase. Probably in ancient times this name was applied to a large vase with a small neck, used for carrying water to the bath. In later archaeological nomenclature, it generally denotes a small vase shaped like a ball, with a short neck and a small orifice surrounded by a broad flat rim, used like the alabastrum in anointing the body with oil.

Athena Nike (a̯-thē′na̯ nī′kē), *Temple of.* Small Ionic amphiprostyle tetrastyle marble temple, dedicated to Athena as goddess of Victory. Pausanias called it the Temple of Nike Apteros or *Wingless Victory;* inscrip-

Temple of Athena Nike
Greek Embassy Press and Information Service

tions indicate that the official designation was as Athena Nike. It was erected c427–424 B.C., on the site of an earlier temple, to designs by Callicrates, one of

fat, fāte, fär, fâll, a̯sk, fāre; net, mē, hėr; pin, pīne; not, nōte, möve, nôr; up, lūte, pu̇ll; oi, oil; ou out; (lightened) e̯lect, agō̯ny, u̯nite;

NIKE LOOSING HER SANDAL, C409 B.C.
Acropolis Museum, Athens
T.A.P. Service

(obscured) errạnt, ardẹnt, actọr; ch, chip; g, go; th, thin; ᵺ, then; y, you;
(variable) ḍ as d or j, ṣ as s or sh, ṭ as t or ch, ẓ as z or zh.

the architects of the Parthenon, and stands at the SW extremity of the Acropolis at Athens on a bastion projecting before the S wing of the Propylaea. Measuring 18 by 27 feet on the stylobate, it has a continuous frieze sculptured in high relief, with an assembly of gods on the E and battle scenes elsewhere. Four slabs of the frieze, among the Elgin Marbles in the British Museum, have been replaced with casts in the reconstructed temple. The small pediments also had sculptures. Along the north, east, and south faces of the bastion was a parapet, the Nike Parapet, sculptured with *Nikai* or Victories in relief, including the famous *Victory Loosing her Sandal,* among the most precious of all Greek sculptures.

The temple was pulled down by the Turks in 1686 to furnish the material for a rampart in front of the Propylaea. In 1834, when this rampart in turn was taken down, the stones of the temple were recovered, and in due course it was rebuilt, but with minor inaccuracies so that in 1936–1941 it was again dismantled and rebuilt. The temple, begun c427 B.C., had been commissioned c449 B.C.; during the interim Callicrates had used the plans in constructing the very similar temple on the Ilissus, which was seen and drawn by Stuart and Revett and was still standing in 1778 but subsequently vanished, torn down presumably for its materials. (JJ)

Athena Parthenos (pär'thẹ-nos). Ivory and gold statue by Phidias, once in the Parthenon. It was one of the most admired works of antiquity. Only copies of the work survive, the most important of which, for its careful reproduction of details, is the Roman copy belonging to the collection of the National Museum at Athens. According to the writer Pausanias (2nd century A.D.), the face, hands, and feet of the image were of ivory; precious stones formed the pupils of the eyes. The robe was of gold. In the image the goddess wore her aegis. On her left side was her shield, on the outside of which was depicted in relief the battle of the Amazons and the Athenians. On the inside of the shield appeared the Battle of the Giants. In her extended right hand the goddess held an image of Victory wearing a golden crown. In her left hand, besides the shield, was her spear. Under the shield was a golden serpent, representing Erichthonius, and on her helmet was the Sphinx. Her sandals were decorated with a scene showing the war between the Centaurs and the Lapiths, and the pedestal showed the birth of Pandora.

Athenodorus (a̧-thē-nọ-dō′rus). Greek sculptor, born at Rhodes; fl. 1st century B.C. He collaborated, according to Pliny the Elder, with Agesander (believed by some to have been his father) and Polydorus on the group of the *Laocoön.*

Athens (ath′ẹnz). [Greek, *Athenai, Athinai;* Latin, *Athenae.*] Capital of Greece, situated about five miles from its seaport Piraeus (on the Saronic Gulf) between the Cephissus and Ilissus rivers on the Attic peninsula. The city lies at 350 feet above sea level on the Attic plain. Surrounding it are the mountains Aegaleos, Parnes, Pentelikon, and Hymettus on the W and E, which sometimes assume at dusk a delicate lavender color and give to the city its epithet "violet-crowned." Within the city limits stands the steep, rocky hill of Lycabettus. The Acropolis, around which the ancient city grew up, rises in the center of the city; it is the site of the earliest settlement and a place of many historical remains. In ancient times, on it were the royal palace and the dwellings of the Eupatrids. To the W is the Areopagus, or Hill of Ares, the site of the most ancient court of Athens, and the place where Saint Paul preached; farther W are the Hill of the Muses, the Pnyx, and the Hill of the Nymphs. In the 5th century B.C. long walls joined the city to its port. The city was founded, according to the old account, by an Egyptian colony led by Cecrops. It became the chief place in Attica, with Athena as its especial divinity, and was ruled by kings, among whom Erechtheus, Theseus, and Codrus are legendary and famous. Gradually the city spread to the lower slopes around the Acropolis and to the banks of the Illisus River. Thither the Eupatrids (nobles) moved and established the ancient aristocratic city described by Thucydides. Besides the Eupatrid enclave, other groups of dwellings to the north and northwest of the Acropolis formed the quarters occupied by artisans and tradesmen, such as the section known as the Ceramicus, alongside the ancient agora which, in the 7th and 6th centuries B.C. became the civic heart of the city. According to tradition, it was Theseus who united the twelve independent communities of Attica into a federal union governed by delegates to Athens. He renamed the Athenian Games the Panathenaea and invited all Attica to share in them, and he united the suburbs mentioned above to the city proper. Furthermore, he invited his fellow Greeks to become Athenian citizens, and many came to Athens. He is said to have divided the population thus enlarged into three classes: the Eupatrids, or nobles; the Georges, or farmers, and the Demiurges, or artisans. Lastly, he gave Athens a constitution, some say, and resigned his throne to further the democracy. After 1132 B.C., the legendary date of the death of Codrus, Athens was ruled by the Eupatrids, and had archons as magistrates, who were successively perpetual, decennial, and (after 683 B.C.) annual. Scholars have questioned the historical value of much of this legendary material. The laws of Draco were enacted in 621 B.C., and those of Solon in 594. Pisistratus became tyrant in 560 B.C. and his sons were expelled in 510. The reforms of Clisthenes (508 B.C.) made Athens (for its day) a pure democracy; popular assemblies of all its citizens (but not all, or even most, of its adult inhabitants were citizens) made the laws. The glorious period began with the Persian wars, in which Athens took a leading part, as at Marathon (490 B.C.) and Salamis

(480). The city was temporarily held by the Persians (480 B.C.) who burned it and destroyed the buildings on the Acropolis. Athens became the head of the Delian League in c477 B.C., and for a short period had an extensive empire and was the first power in Greece. The Athenians in the "Age of Pericles" (c461–429 B.C.) at the onset of the Peloponnesian Wars are described by Thucydides. He puts the following speech into the mouth of the Corinthian envoy who addresses the Spartan assembly considering whether to declare war on Athens:

"You have never considered, O Lacedaemonians, what manner of men are these Athenians with whom you will have to fight, and how utterly unlike yourselves. They are revolutionary, equally quick in the conception and in the execution of every new plan; while you are conservative—careful only to keep what you have, originating nothing, and not acting even when action is most necessary. They are bold beyond their strength; they run risks which prudence would condemn; and in the midst of misfortune they are full of hope. Whereas it is your nature, though strong, to act feebly; when your plans are most prudent, to distrust them; and when calamities come upon you, to think that you will never be delivered from them. They are impetuous and you are dilatory; they are always abroad, and you are always at home. For they hope to gain something by leaving their homes; but you are afraid that any new enterprise may imperil what you have already. When conquerors, they pursue their victory to the utmost; when defeated, they fall back the least. Their bodies they devote to the country as though they belonged to other men; their true self is their mind, which is not truly their own when employed in her service. When they do not carry out an intention which they have formed, they seem to have sustained a personal bereavement; when an enterprise succeeds they have gained a mere installment of what is to come; but if they fail, they at once conceive new hopes and so fill up the void. With them alone to hope is to have, for they lose not a moment in the execution of an idea. This is the lifelong task, full of danger and toil, which they are always imposing upon themselves. None enjoy their good things less, because they are always seeking for more. To do their duty is their only holiday, and they deem the quiet of inaction to be as disagreeable as the most tiresome business. If a man should say of them, in a word, that they were born neither to have peace themselves nor to allow peace to other men, he would simply speak the truth."

In the short period from the victory over the Persians at Marathon (490 B.C.) and Salamis (480), to the defeat of Athens by Sparta (404 B.C.), the tremendous Athenian vitality described by Thucydides produced some of the world's greatest poetry, architecture, and sculpture. At the same time, Athenian commercial and maritime activity predominated in the Mediterranean. The Peloponnesian War (431–404 B.C.) resulted in the displacement of Athens by Sparta in the hegemony of Greece. Athens was defeated by Sparta in 404 B.C. and an aristocratic faction was put in power, but moderate democracy was restored a year later by Thrasybulus. Athens under the influence of Demosthenes resisted Macedonia, but was overthrown at the battle of Chaeronea (338 B.C.), and was generally after this under Macedonian influence. It was subjugated by Rome in 146 B.C., and pillaged by Sulla in 86 B.C.

The ancient architectural masterpieces are mostly on the Acropolis (q.v.), the chief ancient landmark. Other important structures are: the theater of Dionysus on the S slope of the Acropolis, where all the famous Greek dramas were produced. It was originally of wood, and was not completed in stone until the end of the 5th century B.C. The existing remains of the orchestra and stage structures are modifications of Ro-

fat, fāte, fär, fâll, àsk, fâre; net, mē, hèr; pin, pīne; not, nōte, möve, nôr; up, lūte, p*u*ll; oi, oil; ou out; (lightened) ĕlect, agǫny, ūnite;

man date. East, and somewhat south of the Acropolis, are the remains of a temple of Olympian Zeus. According to legend, the first temple on the site was raised by Deucalion, in gratitude for his deliverance from the great flood. About 515 B.C. Pisistratus planned to raise a great temple on the site but the plan was not realized. In the 2nd century B.C., Antiochus IV, king of Syria, revived the plan of building a temple here, but work on it was suspended when he died. It was not until the Roman emperor Hadrian's time that the temple was completed (132 A.D.). Several columns with elaborate Corinthian capitals still stand. Also noteworthy are the

Olympeium
Mary E. Dolbeare

Gate of the Oil Market, or New Agora, a gate built with gifts from Julius Caesar and Augustus; the Agora, to the north of the Acropolis and adjoining the quarter known as Ceramicus. This was the center of Athenian public life and after the Acropolis the heart of the city. Nearly in the center of the Agora was the altar of the

(obscured) errạnt, ardẹnt, actọr; ch, chip; g, go; th, thin; ŦH, then; y, you;
(variable) ḍ as d or j, ṣ as s or sh, ṭ as t or ch, ẓ as z or zh.

Twelve Gods, from which distances from Athens were measured. Among other structures, there were temples of Apollo and of Ares, and an Odeum that held 1000 spectators. Many roads led to the Agora, which was not only the center of Athens but of all Attica. Here were such official buildings as the Bouleterium (Senate), the Tholos, and the Metroun. Here the votes for ostracism were cast. Here were colonnaded galleries for shops and meeting places, the Painted Portico, and various stoas. Public figures, artists, philosophers, and ordinary citizens gathered in the Agora. Religious activity was concentrated about its temples and altars, and through it wound the sacred Panathenaic procession on its way to the Acropolis. Excavations of the site have been carried on at intervals from the 19th century. Since 1931 the American School of Classical Studies has undertaken systematic excavations and restoration on a vast scale. Aided by large grants from John D. Rockefeller Junior and by Marshall Plan funds, and by a law authorizing the demolition of the structures which covered the ancient Agora, the site has been cleared and the excavations of the Agora have shed light on the entire history of Athens, from Neolithic times forward. By 1959 all but the northern side of the Agora had been cleared. The recent excavations had uncovered several 5th century B.C. Ionic columns, remarkable for the good condition of the paint on their capitals, and well-preserved sections of the Panathenaic Roadway, often used for religious processions. In 1970 it was reported that the site of the Royal Stoa, or Stoa of the Basileus, had been unearthed on the Agora. Though completely in ruins, the stoa was estimated to have originally been about 60 feet long and 27 feet wide. It first had a series of Doric columns in front and back, then in the 5th century B.C. further construction gave it columned porches on either side of a large female statue, of which the torso has been found. Named for the *archon basileus* (archon king), this stoa was possibly the site of the trial of Socrates, and stones from the north wall still have the remains of stone benches where some of the judges may have sat. In 1971 the discovery of a nine-foot-by-three-foot limestone slab was reported. Originally placed on the steps of the Royal Stoa, it was possibly the stone on which the nine archons stood to take their oath of office. A museum built on the site of the Agora holds the thousands of objects and coins found in excavations there since 1931. On a slight rise which gives a splendid panoramic view of the Agora stands the well-preserved temple of Hephaestus commonly known as the Theseum. The "Long Walls," traces of which have now almost entirely disappeared, were two massive fortification walls extending from the ramparts of the city to those of the Piraeus, at a distance apart, except near their diverging extremities, of about 550 feet. Built between 461 and 456 B.C., they made the port and the metropolis practically one huge fortress, and assured Athenian supplies by sea while rendering possible Athenian naval triumphs at times when the Spartans held their land without the walls. They were destroyed in 404 B.C. when Athens fell before Sparta but were restored in 393 B.C. by Conon. The Long Walls followed the crests of the group of hills SW of the Acropolis. The arena of the Panathenaic stadium, a stadium still practically complete except for its sheathing of marble, measures 109 by 850 feet, and is bordered on its long sides and its semicircular E end by the slopes which supported the spectators' seats (about 60 tiers). There were at intervals 29 flights of steps to give access to the seats. The original stadium was begun about 330 B.C.; its stone tiers were covered with Pentelic marble through the generosity of Herodus Atticus c143 A.D. In 1895 money was given to restore the stadium in preparation for the Olympic Games of 1896; thus today it gleams with marble not even yet weathered to match other monuments. In

(obscured) errạnt, ardẹnt, actǫr; ch, chip; g, go; th, thin; ꬲH, then; y, you; (variable) ḍ as d or j, ş as s or sh, ṭ as t or ch, ẓ as z or zh.

1958 the discovery of a Cave of Pan about 20 miles E of Athens was reported. Possibly an early place of worship of the Earth Goddess, it then fell into disuse until the Classical Greek period. Inside the cave were found fragments of pottery dating from about 3,500 B.C. to the 2nd century B.C. Roman period. All fragments have been sent to the National Museum in Athens to be studied.

Athlete, The. Greek statue, held to be a copy of the famous Doryphorus (spear-bearer), the canon or type of Polyclitus, found at Pompeii, and added to the collection of the Museo Nazionale, Naples. The undraped figure is well proportioned and holds a simple, naturalistic pose.

——B——

Bassae (bas'ē). Place in Arcadia, Greece, near Phigalia. It is noted for its ruined temple of Apollo Epicurius, built in the second half of the 5th century B.C., probably by Ictinus, the architect of the Parthenon. According to Pausanias, the temple was raised to Apollo Epicurius (*Reliever*) in gratitude to the god for lifting a plague that afflicted the Phigalians during the Peloponnesian War, c420 B.C. Armor found near the temple indicates that Apollo Epicurius may originally have been a war god and shows that the site of his temple on the height (over 3700 feet) was used as a place of refuge for the Phigalians in their wars with Sparta. Set back in the solitude of the mountains of Arcadia, the existence of the temple was forgotten for centuries. It was discovered by a French archaeologist in 1765. According to one account, he overheard an Arcadian shepherd telling a friend that he had left his sheep "up

Temple of Apollo Epicurius
Mary E. Dolbeare

by the pillars." The Frenchman inquired about the "pillars," investigated, and found the temple, one of the best preserved in Greece. It is a Doric peripteros of six by 15 columns, in plan 41 by 125 feet, the cella with pronaos and opisthodomus of two columns *in antis.* In the interior of the cella six piers project from each side wall, their faces formed by Ionic three-quarter columns. A portion toward the back of the cella has no piers, and has a door in the side wall facing the east; it is probable that this was the cella proper, and that the main part of the cella was merely a monumental court, open to the sky—a unique arrangement. The famous frieze, about two feet high (often called the Phigalian Marbles; since 1814 in the British Museum), surrounded the interior of the cella, above the architrave; it is in high relief, and represents combats of Greeks with Amazons and of Lapithae with Centaurs.

Bathycles (bath'i-klēz). Greek sculptor, born at Magnesia (now Manisa, in Turkey), and active probably about the middle of the 6th century B.C. He was commissioned by the Spartans to construct a throne for the colossal image of Amyclaean Apollo in Laconia. On the throne he and his Magnesian assistants carved reliefs representing mythological scenes—Zeus carrying off Taÿgete, Heracles battling Cycnus, the battle of the Centaurs at Pholus, Theseus leading the Cretan Bull, Perseus beheading Medusa, and many more well-known figures of mythology. Under the throne was the tomb of Hyacinthus.

Batrachus (bat'ra̱-kus) or **Batrachos** (-kos). Greek sculptor and architect at Rome in the time of Augustus.

Boëthus (bō-ē'thus). Greek sculptor of the Alexandrian school, born at Chalcedon (or Carthage, according to Pausanias); fl. in the 2nd century B.C. He was famous in antiquity for genre work of a high character. Pliny mentions a bronze figure of a boy strangling a goose, of which there is a replica in the Louvre. The boy extracting a thorn, found in replica in many museums, is supposed to represent Boëthus' statue of the same subject.

Borghese Gladiator (bôr-gā'zā). [Also: **Borghese Warrior, Fighting Gladiator.**] Ancient Greek statue by Agasias of Ephesus, representing a warrior or an athlete. It is in the collection of the Louvre, Paris, having formerly been in the collection of the Villa Borghese, Rome. It dates from late 2nd to early 1st century B.C. The vigorous figure, undraped, is in an attitude of rapid advance, the left arm, encircled by the shield-strap, raised above the head, and the right (restored) extended downward and backward in the line of the body, grasping the sword.

Borghese Mars. Antique statue of Mars in the collection of the Louvre, at Paris.

Bryaxis (brī-ak′sis). Greek sculptor; fl. 4th century B.C. He is best known as one of the four sculptors (the others being Scopas, Leochares, and Timotheus) who created the Mausoleum, the tomb of Mausolus, satrap of Caria, at Halicarnassus, which was completed c333 B.C. The relief panel of the Amazon frieze from the northern face is attributed to Bryaxis. It is believed that Bryaxis was the sculptor of an *Apollo* which stood in the grove of Daphne near Antioch, and other notable ancient works have been attributed to him. A tripod having a base with sculptured figures of horsemen, recovered at Athens in 1891, is shown by its signature to have been his work.

Brygos (brī′gos). Attic potter, active at the beginning of the 5th century B.C. Five vessels signed by him as potter were decorated by the same painter, who became known as the Brygos Painter (because his true name is unknown) and was one of the foremost painters of his time. He has been recognized as the painter of over 170 vessels, chiefly cups. The inside of a cup (Munich) c490 B.C., has a maenad painted in black outline on a white ground. On the outside, in red-figure style, Dionysus appears with a troop of maenads and satyrs. A cup in the Louvre shows an *Iliupersis* (Sack of Troy), and one in the British Museum shows satyrs attacking Iris and Hera. On a cantharus (Boston), Zeus pursues Ganymede; on another (New York), two satyrs relax to music.

BRYAXIS
Battle of Greeks and Amazons, from the N frieze of the Mausoleum at Halicarnassus
British Museum

Calamis (kal′a̯-mis). Greek artist, predecessor of Phidias, who was active at Athens, 480–450 B.C. He was a master of the older style of sculpture, and worked in marble, gold, ivory, and bronze. His works ranged from reliefs on small silver vessels to heroic statues in bronze. Among his works was a group of bronze boys with their hands outstretched, that was dedicated at Olympia. A heroic statue of Apollo at Apollonia in Pontus was carried off to Rome by Lucullus and set up in the Capitol. He was unrivalled for his horses, and produced figures of horsemen and four-horse chariots. The work of Calamis retained some of the archaic stiffness, but also showed an interest in and developing capacity for natural expression.

Callaeschrus (ka̯-lēs′krus). Sixth century B.C. Greek architect, associated with Antistates, Antimachides, and Porinus in preparing the original plans for the Olympieum, the colossal temple of Zeus Olympius at Athens projected by the Pisistratids. (JJ)

Callicrates (ka̯-lik′ra̯-tēz). Athenian architect and sculptor of the 5th century B.C. His great claim to fame is that he was the collaborator of Ictinus in designing the Parthenon on the Acropolis of Athens. He is also known to have designed the much-admired small marble temple of Athena Nike on the Acropolis near the Propylaea, which was completed c424 B.C.

Callimachus (ka̯-lim′a̯-kus). Greek sculptor, active toward the end of the 5th century B.C. He is credited with having originated the Corinthian capital, and with having been first to use the running drill for imitating the deep folds of drapery in statues. He made a golden lamp for the image of Athena on the Acropolis, and over the lamp he placed a bronze palm to draw off the smoke. He claimed to be the first to drill holes through stones, some say, and for the excessive elaboration of his techniques was given the title "Enfeebler of his Art."

Callirrhoë (ka̯-lir′ō̯-ē). Historic fountain at Athens, architecturally adorned and provided with conduits by Pisistratus; the use of its water was prescribed for ceremonial rites. From the earliest study of Athenian topography, this fountain has been identified with the copious spring flowing in the bed of the Ilissus, near the temple of Olympian Zeus. Wilhelm Dörpfeld, however, demonstrated the probability that this identification is incorrect, and that the fountain was in fact situated at the SW angle of the Areopagus, on the border of the Agora. Excavation has revealed a water conduit of the Pisistratid epoch ending at the site indicated, which accords with literary testimony.

Canachus (kan′a̯-kus). Greek sculptor (6th century B.C.), of Sicyon in Achaea. Little is known of his work except that, according to Pausanias, he executed two famous statues of Apollo, one in bronze for the city of Miletus in Asia Minor, and one in cedar for Thebes. The former is represented on some of the coins of Miletus.

Cantharus (kan′tha̯-rus). [Also: *Kantharos*.] In ancient Greece, a wide-mouthed cup or vase, with a foot, and two handles rising above the rim. It was used especially for drinking wine.

Capitoline Museum. One of the chief museums of antiquities of Rome. It was founded in 1471 by Pope Sixtus IV, who presented the papal collections to the Roman people, and designated the Capitol as the place where the art treasures of Rome should be preserved. The museum was greatly enriched by Popes Clement XII and Benedict XIV. The collections now occupy the palace on the left-hand side of the Piazza del Campidoglio, which was built in the 17th century from modified designs of Michelangelo. Among the most noted of the antiquities acquired by the Capitoline Museum are the colossal statue of *Mars* in armor, the *Dying Gaul*, the *Satyr* of Praxiteles, the *Centaurs* by Aristeas and Papias, and the *Capitoline Venus* (after Praxiteles).

Caryae (kar′i-ē). A place in Laconia sacred to Artemis and the nymphs. Here Carya, daughter of a Laconian king died, and the Laconians had the news of her death from Artemis. The Laconians built a temple of Artemis, the columns of which were made in imitation of

Caryatid
Mary E. Dolbeare

(obscured) errạnt, ardẹnt, actọr; ch, chip; g, go; th, thin; ŦH, then; y, you; (variable) ḍ as d or j, ṣ as s or sh, ṭ as t or ch, ẓ as z or zh.

the dancing girls who performed at the annual festivals of Artemis, whence the name "caryatid" by which such columns came to be known (as those of the Erechtheum on the Acropolis at Athens).

Cella (sel′ạ). The room or chamber which formed the nucleus of an ancient Greek or Roman temple and contained the image of the deity, as distinguished from the additional rooms, porticoes, etc., often combined with the cella to form the complete temple.

Cephisodotus (sef-i-sod′ọ-tus). Name of two Greek sculptors, often confused with each other, of the 4th century B.C. One was a relative, possibly the father or a brother, of Praxiteles, and something is known of his work from a copy, at Munich, of a statue of Pluto, or Wealth, as an infant in the arms of Irene, or Peace. The other Cephisodotus was a son of Praxiteles; it is known that he made portrait sculptures, but no examples of his work survive.

Ceramicus (ser-ạ-mī′kus). Large area on the NW side of ancient Athens, Greece, so named from the early gathering in it of potters, attracted by the presence of water and excellent clay. It was divided into parts, the Inner Ceramicus, within the walls, traversed by the Dromos Street from the Dipylon Gate, and including the Agora; and the Outer Ceramicus, continuing the first division outside of the walls. The Outer Ceramicus became a favorite place of burial for the Athenians, and here were interred those honored with a public funeral. The tombs were ranged beside and near the various roads which radiated from the Dipylon Gate. Little trace of them remains, except of the unique group upon and near the inception of the Sacred Way to Eleusis, a group which was preserved by being buried in 86 B.C. in the siege *agger* (earthwork) of Sulla, and contains historical and plastic memorials of very high value, among them the sculptured monument of Dexileus, who fell (393 B.C.) before Corinth, and tombs of Euphrosyne, Hegeso, Aristion, Demetria, and Pamphile.

Chares (kā′rēz, kär′ēz). Rhodian sculptor, born at Lindus, Rhodes; active c292–c280 B.C. He is noted as the creator of the Colossus of Rhodes. He was a pupil of Lysippus and is considered the founder of the Rhodian school. The Colossus of Rhodes was made to commemorate the successful defense of that place against Demetrius I (Demetrius Poliorcetes) in 305 and 304 B.C. It required 12 years for its completion, and was probably finished before 280 B.C. Representing the Rhodian sun-god, Helius, it was over 105 feet high, and was considered one of the seven wonders of the ancient world. Its cost is said to have been defrayed from the engines of war which Demetrius was obliged to abandon.

Chersiphron (kėr′si-fron). Cretan architect, born at Cnossus, Crete, active c576 B.C. He is traditionally considered the designer of the first Artemisium (temple of Artemis) at Ephesus. He was associated with his son Metagenes, and with Theodorus. The Artemisium was more than 100 years in building, and was finished c456 B.C. It was later destroyed by fire, and rebuilt about the time of Alexander the Great by Dinocrates; this building, usually called the Temple of Diana of Ephesus, was one of the seven wonders of the ancient world.

Cimon of Cleonae (sī′mon; klē-ō′nē). Greek painter, born at Cleonae, in Chalcidice, famous in antiquity. He is mentioned in two epigrams of Simonides.

Clearchus (klē-är′kus). Greek sculptor of Rhegium, who was active c540–500 B.C. He is said to have made the first image in bronze. According to Pausanias, it was an image of Zeus, made in several pieces, and fastened together with nails. This image was in Sparta. According to legend, Clearchus was a pupil of Daedalus.

Cleitias (klī′ti-as). [Also: *Kleitias*.] Attic vase-painter in the black-figure style, active in the second quarter of the

(obscured) errant, ardent, actor; ch, chip; g, go; th, thin; ᴛʜ, then; y, you;
(variable) ḍ as d or j, ṣ as s or sh, ṭ as t or ch, ẓ as z or zh.

6th century B.C. The François vase (c570 B.C.), named for its finder and now in Florence, is an amphora signed by Cleitias as the painter and Ergotimus as the potter. There are more than 200 figures on the vase, many of which are identified by inscribed names. The scenes of the decoration include the *Calydonian Hunt, Funeral Games for Patroclus, Procession of the gods to the Marriage of Thetis and Peleus, Achilles Pursuing Troilus, Hephaestus Returning to Olympus, Ajax Carrying the Body of Achilles, Battle of the Pygmies and Cranes,* and various monsters. A stand in New York and various extant cups also bear the signatures of Cleitias and Ergotimus as painter and potter respectively.

Cleophrades (klē-of'rạ-dēz). Attic potter, active at the beginning of the 5th century B.C. The painter who deco-

CLEOPHRADES PAINTER
Maenad, red-figured amphora, c500 B.C.
Munich

rated his work, in the red-figure style, is known as the Cleophrades Painter. Over 100 large vessels—cra-

ters and hydriai—attributed to the Cleophrades
Painter are extant. Of these, there are nine Panathenaic amphorae (the ceremonial vessels awarded at
the great festival), in the traditional black-figure style.
Two calyx craters (New York and Tarquinia) show
youths arming. An amphora (Munich) c500 B.C., shows
Dionysus with maenads and satyrs on the body of the
vessel, and scenes of the palestra on the neck. Of two
more amphorae in Munich one shows the departure of
a warrior and scenes of the palestra in red-figure, with
a hunting scene on the rim of the vessel and a chariot
race on the lid, in black-figure. The other amphora has
a figure of Heracles on one side, prepared to do battle
with the centaur on the other side. An amphora (New
York) similarly decorated with a single figure on each
side shows Apollo raising his bow on one side, against
Heracles, who is carrying off the Delphic tripod on the
other. A hydria (Naples) has an *Iliupersis* (Sack of
Troy). The Cleophrades Painter, known by that name
for lack of knowledge as to his real name for a long
time, has been identified by his real name, Epictetus,
but is not to be confused with the vase-painter Epictetus who lived a generation earlier.

Cnossus or *Knossos* (nos'us). [Also: *Cnosus, Gnossus,
Gnosus.*] In ancient geography, the capital of Crete, on
the north coast and in the eastern half of the island. It
was the site of a series of fabulous Minoan palaces. The
site was discovered, 1886, by Heinrich Schliemann but
he was unable to obtain the property at a price he
considered fair, and abandoned his plan to excavate it.
Sir Arthur Evans, the English archaeologist, visited the
island in 1894, subsequently acquired the site of Cnossus, and began his excavations in 1900. His finds there
were only equalled in importance by the earlier discoveries of Schliemann at Mycenae. The area of the palaces constructed at Cnossus was a low hill, in the valley
of the Caeratus River. The discovery of wooden and
bone utensils of the Neolithic Age showed that the site

had been occupied since c3000 B.C. In succeeding ages two great palaces were erected at the site, the second of which was rebuilt after being partially destroyed. The first great palace was built about 2000 B.C. It was destroyed, by unknown means, c1700 B.C. Immediately a new and grander palace was erected on the ruins. The second palace was badly damaged, c1600 B.C., and was reconstructed, on a less extensive scale, in succeeding years. When, c1400 B.C., this palace too was destroyed, perhaps by an earthquake or by a sudden enemy raid, the site was thereafter only sparsely occupied. The second Minoan palace is the one associated with King Minos, Pasiphaë, the Minotaur, and the exploits of Theseus. The palaces were built on several levels connected by stairways and without any particular plan. Around a large central court groups of separate buildings were clustered. As more buildings were added, light and air were admitted to them by secondary courts and porticoes. With the passage of time, the buildings were connected by corridors to link them all into the complex that formed the palace. The builders were less concerned with the outside symmetry of the palace than with the comfort within it, and added chambers, courts, and porticoes with their connecting corridors as they were required, with the result that the corridors linking various parts of the palace, the stairways by which different levels were approached, and the series of courts and porticoes, made it into a perfect maze. The double-ax, the word for which was *labrys,* was a symbol of power, as well as a religious symbol and a mason's mark. It appeared in many places throughout the palace marked on walls and vessels, and double-axes were found in the chamber that came to be known as the "Room of the Double-Axes." The ending *-nth,* not of Greek origin, means "place of." Hence the palace was called *Labyrinth,* "place of the double-ax," but because of its mazelike arrangement the word "labyrinth" came to be thought of in succeeding years as a "maze." It may well be, therefore, that the story of Theseus and the Minotaur refers to the success Theseus enjoyed in the sport of bull-leaping in the central court around which the Labyrinth, "place of the double-ax," was built.

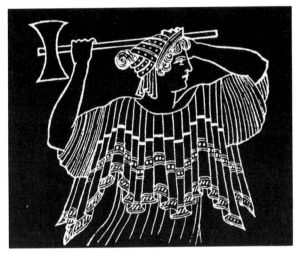

DOUBLE AX
Red-figured Greek vase

Captives were commonly trained to take part in this sport, which consisted in baiting a huge bull. At the moment when the animal lowered its head and charged, the performer seized both its horns, turned a somersault over its head, and landed on the animal's back or on the ground behind it. Engravings on gems and other representations of the sport form a vivid basis for the story of Theseus. A small frescoed panel gives a complete picture of the sport. One of the paved courts of the palace is called the dancing-floor that was built for Ariadne by Daedalus.

Rather than attempt an ordered description of the conglomeration of courts, offices, magazines, baths, royal quarters, domestic quarters, treasure chambers, services areas, etc., it must suffice to mention some of the outstanding features of the palaces that sprawled on the hill at Cnossus. The outer walls were of stone or stone facing. The inner walls were of plaster and were decorated with richly colored frescoes. The frescoes have given valuable knowledge of the dress, life, and ceremonials of the times. They have also given names to some of the areas of the palace. A long corridor on the west is called the "Corridor of the Procession," from the fresco showing slim-waisted

PROCESSION OF THE YOUNG MEN
Restoration, Palace at Cnossus, c1600 B.C.

men, clad in loin cloths, bearing sacred vessels on their heads, and marching in a trim line across the wall. Another fresco shows an audience, including women, watching the sport of bull-leaping; and still another portrays elegant, black-haired ladies of the royal court. Wooden pillars, tapering from the top down and painted a rich terra-cotta color with blue bands at the

fat, fāte, fär, fåll, åsk, fāre; net, mē, hėr; pin, pīne; not, nōte, möve, nôr; up, lūte, pùll; oi, oil; ou out; (lightened) ēlect, agǫny, ūnite;

top, rested on stone bases and supported the roofs and floors of the different levels. Water was brought from the hills by a "siphon" system and distributed through the palace by terra-cotta pipes and stone ducts. The supply was augmented by collecting rain-water from the roofs in shafts and causeways. Light and air were provided by light wells, covered shafts with openings cut into the walls below the roofs. Light and air were also provided by using the roof of one level as a portico for the next one. The great central court, lying N-S on the hill, was the center about which the rest of the palace was clustered. Just off it, on the west side, is a small chamber that has been named the throne room because in it, against the middle of one wall, a gypsum chair with rounded seat and high back was found. This is called the throne of Minos. On each side of it are stone benches for the royal visitors. The walls of the throne room were frescoed in strong colors with images of griffins and stylized vegetation. Opposite the throne is a sunken chamber, similar to others throughout the palace, that was probably used for purification rites. Its position so close to the throne indicates the close connection between the religious and temporal power of the king. To the east, the hill on which the palace stands drops away sharply. Here some of the underground rooms of the royal quarters have been preserved in their entirety, such as the Queen's Apartments, with blue-green dolphins leaping and playing on the frescoed walls. Four flights of the grand stairway that led down to the royal apartments have been preserved. This is a most noble and serenely proportioned structure. Short flights, carefully designed for dignified ascent and set at right angles to each other, rise up the stair well. Pillars set on stone balustrades form an outer rail and add to the beauty of the structure. Ranged throughout the palace, on varying levels, are magazines under the protection of the double ax, where oil and grain were stored. Huge earthenware

(obscured) errạnt, ardẹnt, actọr; ch, chip; g, go; th, thin; ŦH, then; y, you; (variable) ḍ as d or j, ṣ as s or sh, ṭ as t or ch, ẓ as z or zh.

storage jars still stand as they were left thousands of years ago. Some of the magazines were used for the storage of treasure, judging by the bits of gold leaf that were found in them. Others were used for the sacred

Storage jar *(pithos) in situ* at Cnossus

vessels belonging to the snake-goddess. Workshops containing fine painted pottery, unfinished stone vases, and material for producing other objects, were located in the north end of the east wing of the palace. Gathered about the palace were luxurious private villas that shared such features of the palace as light-wells, plumbing, porches, and lively frescoes. To the south of the palace, across a little stream, there are the remains of an inn that housed distant visitors to the

fat, fāte, fär, fåll, ȧsk, fãre; net, mē, hėr; pin, pīne; not, nõte, möve, nôr; up, lūte, půll; oi, oil; ou out; (lightened) ēlect, agǫny, ūnite;

palace. Cnossus was the center of a network of roads
that radiated out over the eastern end of the island.
The palace was unfortified, attesting to the unchal-
lenged supremacy of Minoan sea power, as the richness of the palace, its comfort, and the highly
developed techniques that built and furnished it attest
to the brilliance of the Minoan civilization. Sir Arthur
Evans, to whom the world is indebted for the evidences
of this brilliant civilization, made a series of partial
restorations of the palace. Following such clues as his
excavations gave him he restored some of the frescoes,
as that in the Corridor of the Procession (the original
pieces of the fresco are in the Museum). Richly painted
pillars were set up in certain places to restore porches
and porticoes and more importantly, to replace the
debris that was all that held up some of the upper
floors. His restorations of porches, pillars, light-wells,
and frescoes in several areas give a vivid impression of
the style of architecture and decoration of the Minoan
civilization, so different from those of the Classical
Greek period. The tombs of many of the royal inhabitants of Cnossus were located on a hill about 10 miles
southeast of the palace. Most of the tombs have long
since been plundered, but in 1966 the discovery of an
intact tomb was reported. The 3,250-year-old burial
place of a queen, it had partially caved in but was kept
from grave-robbers by a wall sealing it off from the
other tombs. The burial chamber contained a terra-
cotta sarcophagus, standing two-and-a-half feet high
on legs and painted in a papyrus-leaf motif. About 120
gold objects, most of them dating from the Greek period in Crete after 1400 B.C., were found in the sarcophagus. Jewelry buried with the queen included a gold
cylinder for her hair; eight necklaces, three of gold
beads and five of semi-precious stones; and five gold
rings. One of these rings, dating from before 1400
B.C., is delicately carved with a worship scene and is
possibly the finest signet ring of this period ever found

on Crete. Evidences of the burial ceremony included ceremonial vessels found in the tomb and the head of the queen's horse buried in the wall sealing the tomb.

Colossus of Rhodes (kǫ-los′us; rōdz). Large bronze statue of the sun god Helius, which anciently stood adjacent to the harbor of Rhodes on the Greek island of that name. Known in ancient and medieval times as one of the Seven Wonders of the World, it was designed by Chares of Lindus, and under his supervision erected between 292 and 280 B.C. It is reputed to have been 70 cubits high, or more than 100 feet, and is said to have been built from the abandoned bronze weapons and armor left by the soldiers of Demetrius I, king of Macedon, when they retired in defeat from their siege of Rhodes. The tradition that ships could sail between the colossal legs is erroneous. In 224 B.C. it was toppled by an earthquake. For many centuries great bronze fragments of the statue lay where they fell.

Colotes (kol-ō′tēz). Greek sculptor, a pupil of Phidias, who worked with him on the great statue of Olympian Zeus. He also made the table on which rested the victors' crowns at Olympia.

Corinth (kôr′inth, kor′-). [Also: *Gortho;* Greek, *Korinthos;* Latin, *Corinthia, Corinthus;* ancient name: *Ephyra.*] City "in the corner of Argos" in the Peloponnesus, situated near the Isthmus and Gulf of Corinth. According to tradition, it was founded c1350 B.C., some say by Sisyphus. Poseidon and Helius contended for control of Corinthia, and Briareus acted as arbitrator of their dispute. He awarded the Isthmus and adjoining land to Poseidon, and the height above the city (the Acrocorinthus) to Helius. Thereafter, the Isthmus was sacred to Poseidon, who had a temple there in which were altars and images of various sea-deities. The body of Melicertes, son of Ino and Athamas, was washed ashore on the Isthmus and buried there, and Isthmian Games were established in his honor. The graves of Sisyphus and Neleus were on the Isthmus, but their

fat, fāte, fär, fâll, àsk, fāre; net, mē, hèr; pin, pīne; not, nōte, möve, nôr; up, lūte, pùll; oi, oil; ou out; (lightened) ēlect, agǫny, ūnite;

exact whereabouts was a well-kept secret. The region was also the scene of some of the exploits of Theseus. Theseus, Poseidon, and Corinthus represent the original Ionian inhabitants of Corinthia. Sisyphus, Jason, and Neleus represent the Aeolians who immigrated there. Cenchreae was the east port and Lechaeum was the west port of the Isthmus. A coin of the time of the emperor Hadrian represents the two harbors as two nymphs facing opposite ways with a rudder between them. In ancient times, ships were sometimes placed on rollers and dragged across the Isthmus, to save the long voyage around the Peloponnesus. Periander, tyrant of Corinth (c625–585 B.C.), planned to breach the Isthmus with a canal, but gave up the idea. Much later, the emperor Nero began to cut a canal, but he too abandoned the project. (The existing canal was completed in 1893). In the Persian Wars, the Peloponnesians, under the leadership of Sparta, built a wall across the Isthmus as a fortification against the Persians. Some say the land about the Asopus River, in the NE corner of the Peloponnesus, was divided by Helius between his son Aeëtes to whom he gave Ephyraea (ancient name for Corinthia), and Aloeus to whom he gave Sicyonia. Aeëtes migrated to Colchis and left his kingdom in trust with Bunus, son of Hermes. After the death of Bunus the kingdom fell successively to the rule of Epopeus, then to his son Marathon, and then to his grandson Corinthus, for whom the name of the city was changed from Ephyra to Corinth. Corinthus died childless just at the time when Medea arrived from Colchis with Jason. She claimed the throne for Jason. Some say that when she was forced to flee from Corinth, she gave her kingdom to Sisyphus. His descendants were ruling when the Dorians invaded the Peloponnesus in the 11th century B.C., defeated the Corinthians, and expelled them. The Dorian rulers were followed by Bacchis (926–891 B.C.) and his descendants, the Bacchiadae, who were overthrown by

(obscured) errant, ardent, actor; ch, chip; g, go; th, thin; ᴛʜ, then; y, you;
(variable) ḍ as d or j, ş as s or sh, ṭ as t or ch, ẓ as z or zh.

Cypselus c657 B.C. The city of Corinth was well supplied with water. According to tradition, the river-god
Asopus gave Sisyphus the never-failing Pirene spring

Pirene Spring

in return for information about the whereabouts of
one of his daughters, Aegina. It was at this spring that
Athena bridled Pegasus for Bellerophon. In memory
of the event, a temple of Athena Chalinitis *(Bridler)*,
was raised. The well of Glauce at Corinth was said to
be the one in which Glauce, daughter of Creon, flung
herself to get relief from the burning poison of the
robe Medea had sent her. Nearby the well was the
tomb of Medea's children. Some say they were stoned
to death by the Corinthians in revenge for the death of

fat, fāte, fär, fåll, àsk, fāre; net, mē, hėr; pin, pīne; not, nōte, mŏve,
nôr; up, lūte, půll; oi, oil; ou out; (lightened) ĕlect, agọny, ūnite;

Glauce. Afterward the Corinthians were punished until, at the command of the oracle, they offered annual sacrifices in honor of the dead children and set up a figure of Terror. As they were subject to Argos and Mycenae, the Corinthians had no leader in the Trojan War, but took part in it under the command of Agamemnon.

CORINTHIAN JUG, 7TH CENTURY B.C.

Corinth was noted in ancient times as a center of commerce, literature, and art, and as one of the wealthiest and most powerful of the ancient Greek cities. It sent colonies to Corcyra (Corfu) and Syracuse in 734 B.C., and founded Potidaea in Chalcidice and Apollonia on the coast of Epirus. During the rule of Periander (c625–585 B.C.), son of Cypselus, Corinth had reached a peak of cultural and commercial prosperity. The rise of Athens following the Persian Wars threat-

ened the commercial supremacy of Corinth. A struggle
over the Corinthian city of Potidaea, which was a tributary ally of Athens, was one of the precipitating causes
of the Peloponnesian Wars, in which Corinth sided
with Sparta against Athens. The alliance with Sparta
disintegrated after the defeat of Athens in the Peloponnesian Wars, and Corinth engaged (395–387 B.C.)
in the "Corinthian War" against Sparta. It was defeated by Sparta in 394 B.C. It later fell to the
Macedonians and was held by them until 243 B.C.,
when it joined the Achaean League of which it was the
capital. In 146 B.C. it was captured, sacked, and burned
by the Romans, under Mummius; it was rebuilt by
Julius Caesar in 46 B.C. Pausanias visited the rebuilt

Temple of Apollo, 7th century B.C.
Greek National Tourist Office

city in the 2nd century A.D. and has left descriptions of
the monuments of the restored city. He tells, for example, of an image of Dionysus in the market-place that
was supposed to have been made from the tree from
which Pentheus spied on the maenads as they celebrated their revels, and from which he was dragged to

his death. He mentions a temple of Palaemon (the name by which Melicertes was known when he became a god), and of Aphrodite Melaenis *(Black)*. Still to be seen are the ruins of an archaic temple of Apollo, a Roman theater, an odeum, the agora with basilicas, colonnades, a hostelry, fountains, and other public buildings, the Fountain of Pirene, and much besides, excavated since the 1890's by the American School of Classical Studies at Athens.

Corinthian Order (kō-rin'thi-ạn). In architecture, the most ornate of the classical orders, and the most slender in its proportions. The capital is shaped like a bell, adorned with rows of acanthus leaves, and less commonly with leaves of other plants. The usual form of abacus (q.v.) is concave on each of its sides, the pro-

CORINTHIAN COLUMN

jecting angles being supported by graceful shoots of acanthus, forming volutes which spring from stalks originating among the foliage covering the lower part of the capital. These stalks also give rise to lesser stalks and to spirals turned toward the middle, and supporting an anthemion or other ornament in the middle of each side of the abacus. In the best Greek examples, the shaft is fluted like the Ionic, and the base called Attic is usual. The entablature also resembles the Ionic. The Corinthian order is of very early origin, though it did not come into favor among the Greeks until comparatively late. The legend of the evolution of the Corinthian capital by Callimachus, in the 5th century B.C., from a *calathus* (woman's basket) placed on a maiden's tomb and covered with a tile, about which the leaves of a plant of acanthus had grown, is a fable. Among notable Greek examples of the order are the Tholos of Polyclitus at Epidaurus (5th century B.C.), the choragic monument of Lysicrates at Athens (c335 B.C.), and the temple of the Olympian Zeus at Athens (columns of which are a feature of the Athenian landscape), finished by the emperor Hadrian. The rich character of the order commended it to the Romans, who used it freely, and modified it in accordance with their taste.

Cossutius (ko̞-sö′shus). Roman architect, engaged by the Seleucid emperor Antiochus IV Epiphanes (175–164 B.C.) to prepare new designs and resume construction, in the Corinthian order, of the vast temple of Zeus Olympius at Athens, which had been begun as a Doric temple by the Pisistratids in the 6th century B.C. and abandoned on the exiling of Hippias in 510 B.C. On Antiochus' death construction was halted again and the temple was completed only c132 A.D. during the reign of the Roman emperor Hadrian. The employment of a Roman to design a major Greek temple has been taken to indicate that Cossutius was an architect of extraordinary ability, or that he was really a Greek who had gained Roman citizenship and name. (JJ)

Crater (krā′tėr). [Also: *Krater.*] In ancient Greece, a large vessel or vase in which, as was Greek custom, water was mixed with wine according to accepted formulas, and from which it was dipped out and served to the guests in the smaller pouring-vessels *(oinochoë)*. There are at least three types of craters. The bell crater is open and bell-like, with a foot, and a small handle placed very low on either side. The column crater, also footed, curves inward near the top to form a shoulder from which rises a neck of somewhat smaller diameter that ends in a rim; the handles rise as columns from the shoulder of the vessel to the rim. The volute crater, also footed, and like the column crater ending in a neck, has handles that rise from the shoulder and curl in a volute well above the rim. Many beautiful examples, richly decorated, are preserved.

CALYX CRATER
Theseus and the Marathonian Bull, 440–430 B.C.
The Metropolitan Museum of Art

Cresilas (kres′i-las). Greek sculptor; born at Cydonia, Crete; active in the second half of the 5th century B.C. His career was made at Athens, where he was a contemporary of Phidias, and where he executed a portrait

(obscured) errant, ardent, actor; ch, chip; g, go; th, thin; ᴛʜ, then; y, you;
(variable) d as d or j, s as s or sh, t as t or ch, z as z or zh.

statue of Pericles. Copies exist of a figure of a wounded Amazon, which Cresilas carved at Ephesus in a competition with Phidias and Polyclitus.

Crete (krēt). [Also: *Candia;* Greek, *Kriti, Krete;* French, *Crète, Candie;* Italian and Latin, *Creta;* Old Turkish, *Kirid, Kirit.*] Island in the Mediterranean Sea, situated SE of Greece and SW of Asia Minor. It has an area of 3235 square miles, is 160 miles long, and 35 miles wide in its greatest width. Sharply rising mountain ridges separate the parts of the island from each other. The mountain slopes, once covered with cedar and cypress, are now largely bare. In the fertile plains and river valleys wheat, fruit, wool, olives, and wine are produced. According to legend, the inhabitants of Crete sprang from the soil. Their first king was Cres, for whom the island was named. Some say the Idaean Dactyls, who discovered the use of fire and metal-working, were born in Crete. The nine Curetes, either sprung from the earth or born of the Dactyls, originated in Crete, and the Titans, especially during the Golden Age of Cronus when men lived like gods, were associated with the island. In a cave on Mount Ida the Curetes protected the infant Zeus by clashing their shields to drown out his cries, while nymphs nourished him with milk and honey. To memorialize the contribution of the bees Zeus changed their color to copper that gleamed like gold in the sun, and made them impervious to changes in the weather, an important consideration in Crete. Athena was said by some to have been born from the head of Zeus at the source of the Triton River in Crete, where a temple was raised to her. The marriage of Zeus and Hera was also said by some to have taken place on the island. Cretans annually reënacted the ceremony at a temple that commemorated this event. Teucer, the ancestor of the Trojans, came from Crete, and Minos, Daedalus, Pasiphaë, the Minotaur, and many other figures of mythology and legend are associated with the island. Long

before the Greeks on the mainland had developed
their ideas of the great god Zeus, however, the Cretans
had elaborated their own concepts of the gods. The
chief figure in their worship was the Great Mother,
who had power over life and death, who was the goddess of the forest and of wild beasts, and who occupied
the central place in Cretan religion. Her attributes
were the double ax, the *labrys,* a symbol of power, and
the Horns of Consecration, which may have been connected with the bull, an animal that appears later in
connection with the story of Europa. The Great
Mother was a triple goddess, who ruled in heaven, on
earth, and under the earth. The animals sacred to her
came from each of her kingdoms—the dove from the
air, the bull or lion from the earth, and the snakes from
the underworld. Joined to the Great Mother was a male
figure, a son-husband, he who was first named Zagreus
by the Greeks and later developed by them into the
great sky-god Zeus, whom the Cretans claimed was
born on their island. They also claimed his tomb in the
hill of Iuctas, the outline of which appears to be a giant
lying on his back, pointing his great bearded profile at
the sky. It was because the Cretans claimed to have the
tomb of Zeus that the Greeks called them "liars," and
gave them a bad reputation throughout the Greek
world. Obviously, Zeus, being a god, could not have
died and been placed in a tomb. Because Crete was
subject to frequent earthquakes, there was a strong
chthonic element to Cretan religion. The Cretans ex-
plained the earthquakes as the tossing of the earth on
the great bull's horns, and propitiated him by offering
him sacrifices of bulls.

The Cretans are thought to be of Libyan or
Anatolian stock. Homer names them as Achaeans,
Cydonians, Dorians, Pelasgians, and Eteocretans, the
last of whom are believed to be the original non-Hel-
lenic inhabitants. But Homer wrote long after the
greatest ages of Cretan civilization had passed away.

(obscured) errạnt, ardẹnt, actọr; ch, chip; g, go; th, thin; ꬲн, then; y, you;
(variable) ḍ as d or j, ṣ as s or sh, ṭ as t or ch, ʐ as z or zh.

Cretan civilization existed before 3000 B.C., and was in a continuous state of development thereafter, reaching its height in the period 3000–1400 B.C. The German archaeologist Heinrich Schliemann believed that Crete was the legendary isle of Atlantis. He thought Crete might be the origin of the highly developed art he had found in Greece. He discovered the site of the palace of Cnossus in 1886, but was unable to carry out his plan for excavating it. It remained for Sir Arthur Evans the British archaeologist, who had visited the island in 1894, to acquire the site and, in 1900, to begin his excavations. Other excavations in various parts of the island have been carried on by the Italians, by the French School, the English School, by Americans, and by the Greeks. Sir Arthur Evans classified the distinctive periods into which Cretan civilization falls according to ceramic development, as follows:

Early Minoan	I (E.M.I.)		3400–2800 B.C.
"	"	II (E.M.II)	2800–2400 B.C.
"	"	III (E.M.III)	2400–2100 B.C.
Middle Minoan	I (M.M.I.)		2100–1900 B.C.
"	"	II (M.M.II)	1900–1700 B.C.
"	"	III (M.M.III)	1700–1580 B.C.
Late Minoan	I (L.M.I.)		1580–1450 B.C.
"	"	II (L.M.II)	1450–1375 B.C.
"	"	III (L.M.III)	1375–1100 B.C.

The relatively strict dates for each period are possible because of close synchronization with Egyptian history, for Cretan external relations were oriented toward Egypt from an early date. Habitations have been discovered beneath the palaces of Cnossus (q.v.) and Phaestus that date from the Neolithic Age, before 3000 B.C. Wooden and bone utensils, and polished and incised pottery of this period have been found on these and other sites. In the period from 3000–2000 B.C. two great centers of civilization developed, that around the plain of Mesara, on the southern side of the island, and that at the eastern end of the island. In this period

fat, fāte, fär, fåll, åsk, fãre; net, mē, hėr; pin, pīne; not, nōte, möve, nôr; up, lūte, pùll; oi, oil; ou out; (lightened) ėlect, agŏny, ŭnite;

close commercial relations were held with the islands of the Cyclades, with Egypt, and with Asia Minor. This period saw the development of gray incised pottery, decorated with simple figures—zig-zags, herringbones, groups of parallel lines, and rows of dots (E.M.I); pottery decorated with red and black on a natural clay ground (E.M.II); and pottery painted in white on a black glazed ground on which new patterns were introduced (E.M.III). Also in this period, great progress was made in metal-working and in the art of carving stone vases, employing the natural strata of the stone as decoration. In the Middle Minoan periods the polychrome style, called "Kamares ware" (because first examples of it were found by the English in a cave at Kamares, on the south slope of Mount Ida) was developed, with white, red, and yellow decorations on a black glazed ground. By the Middle Minoan periods I and II (2100–1700 B.C.), a brilliant civilization had evolved. The first palaces were built at Cnossus and Phaestus; the polychrome Kamares ware had become highly decorative with stylized figures, such as the octopus motif; and the refinement developed in the techniques of the potter's wheel led to the production of "egg-shell" vases, so named for their thinness, with fluted bodies and rims of great delicacy. A system of hieroglyphic writing was in use; commercial relations in the Aegean were widened, continued with Egypt, and extended into Asia. At the end of this era of the fabulous development of a civilization far in advance of any that had developed on the Greek mainland at this time, some unknown catastrophe struck all the centers of Cretan civilization and destroyed them, about 1700 B.C. The interruption was temporary. Between 1700 and 1400 B.C. new and grander palaces were raised at Cnossus, Phaestus, and Mallia; comfortable private houses with oiled parchment for window panes were built around the palaces; new cities were founded; relations with Egypt and the Near East flourished; and

Cretan colonies were sent out to the neighboring islands and to the Greek mainland. Cretan civilization and power was at its height. The age was characterized by the figure of King Minos, who had the largest and most powerful navy in existence and controlled the waters of the Mediterranean. Some say that the name "Minos" was a title similar to the Egyptian word "Pharaoh," and that it applied to at least two Cretan kings, and perhaps to a series of them. Palaces and houses were decorated inside and out with brilliantly colored frescoes that depicted naturalistic scenes, such

SNAKE GODDESS
Faience statuette from the Palace at Cnossus, 1600–1580 B.C.
Heraklion

as the human figure, sacrificial processions, and religious gatherings, thus recording much of the Cretan way of life. Sculptured stone vases, decorated pottery jars, some of great size, and golden cups worked in relief with consummate artistry, were in use in the palaces. Fragile vases and delicate figurines played a part in religious ceremonies or served for ornamentation. The king and others had exquisite seals cut in gems for sealing their documents. Seal engraving was developed to perfection in the Middle Minoan and following periods. Animals at rest and in action, birds in flight, human figures, were engraved with exquisite grace and fidelity on ivory, steatite, crystal, jasper, and other hard surfaces. From the miniature seal engravings of ceremonial scenes comes much of our knowledge of Minoan ritual. Relief decorations on cups and carving reached a peak of refinement. These are exemplified by the famous Vaphio cups (so-called because they were found at Vaphio, near Sparta, whither they had been carried from Crete), with their scenes of the bull hunt and of the bulls in pasture beautifully worked in repoussé, and by the extraordinary figure of the bull-leaper carved in ivory. Frescoes show large audiences, including women, watching the sport of bull-leaping, which differed from the bull-fight in that the performer must catch the horns of the bull as the animal charged, leap over its head, and land on his feet on its back. Many scenes and stories, as well as religious ceremonies, centered about the bull. Two styles of linear writing were in use in this period—the Linear Script A and Linear Script B—and indicated that the Cretans had an alphabet long before Cadmus introduced the Phoenician alphabet into Greece. The Linear Script B was deciphered, half a century after the first examples of it had been found, by the Englishman Michael Ventris, in 1952. In 1957 Prof. Cyrus H. Gordon of Brandeis University announced that an adaptation of Accadian was the language of the Linear Script

(obscured) errạnt, ardẹnt, actọr; ch, chip; g, go; th, thin; ᴛн, then; y, you;
(variable) ḍ as d or j, ṣ as s or sh, ṭ as t or ch, ẓ as z or zh.

A. In the houses and palaces of this era brilliant use of "light-wells" was made for ventilation and illumination; ingenious "siphon systems" brought water from the hills to the palaces, where it was then distributed by means of terra-cotta pipes and stone ducts. The household water supply was also augmented by rain

Storage jars *(pithoi) in situ,* and magazines, Palace at Cnossus

water drained from the roofs. This period, so briefly described, was the era of Cretan supremacy, in commercial and maritime power, and in the refinement and brilliance of its civilization. About 1400 B.C. general catastrophe overcame the flourishing civilization and destroyed it, apparently at once. Some think it must have been a great natural disaster, as an earthquake, that put such a sudden end to the great palaces and Minoan cities. Others think it was perhaps a swooping raid by Achaeans from the mainland that utterly overthrew the Cretan civilization. The Athenian legend is that Theseus caused the overthrow of Cretan civilization, for when he fled with Ariadne,

fat, fāte, fär, fåll, ȧsk, fãre; net, mē, hėr; pin, pīne; not, nōte, möve, nôr; up, lūte, půll; oi, oil; ou out; (lightened) ẹlect, agǫny, ūnite;

the Cretan fleet pursued him and in its absence the island was beset by enemies. Others say the island was exposed to raiders when King Minos sailed off in his fleet to recover Daedalus, who had escaped on waxen wings to the kingdom of Cocalus in Sicily. In the following centuries, 1400–1100 B.C., Crete was dominated by the Mycenaean culture. Its own became decadent, the palatial sites were not reoccupied to any great extent; the importance of Crete as a center of art, culture, and commerce declined completely. Homer mentions in the *Iliad* that Crete, "century-citied," sent soldiers against Troy under the leadership of Idomeneus and Meriones. In the *Odyssey* he describes the palace of Alcinous, with its gold and silver doors, and its decorations of blue enamel, and though some think the island home of Alcinous was Corcyra or Corfu, the description of the palace might equally well apply to the palaces of Crete. After the time of the Trojan War the "hundred cities" of Crete warred so among themselves that they became an easy prey for the Dorians, who invaded their island, c1100 B.C., and put a period to the Minoan civilization. At the beginning of the era that culminated in the Classical period, c750 B.C., Cretan culture enjoyed a renascence. Cretan archaic art and skilled craftsmanship, heirs of the master smith Daedalus, influenced developments on the Greek mainland. Independent cities coined their own money, and it was in this time that the famous Gortynian Code of Laws was promulgated—an extraordinary document that detailed all kinds of social and economic laws, and was engraved on the walls of a portico or arcade near Gortyna. Crete played no role in the Persian and Peloponnesian Wars. Its relations with the mainland were slight. By the height of the great Classical period its artistic developments had come to a halt. Its age of greatness was far in the past. In 66 B.C. the island fell, but not without difficulty, under the domination of the Romans. In 1963 it was reported that

(obscured) err*a*nt, ard*e*nt, act*o*r; ch, chip; g, go; th, thin; ᴛʜ, then; y, you; (variable) ḏ as d or j, ṣ as s or sh, ṯ as t or ch, ẓ as z or zh.

ruins of a palace destroyed about 1450 B.C. had been discovered at Kato Zakro, in eastern Crete. The palace was originally built to the height of two to three stories around a central courtyard and held ceremonial halls and banquet rooms as well as extensive private apartments for royalty. Excavations of the ruins have yielded several major finds, including the only capital of a Minoan pillar ever found on Crete, twelve tablets in Linear Script A, and a 19-inch-wide bronze double-ax of a type previously known only from carvings of ceremonial scenes. Other finds, now in the Archaeological Museum of Herakleion (Heracleum), include religious vessels, many carved from imported stone, fluted drinking vessels and jars, lamps, ritual mallets, copper money, a nine-inch bronze mirror, painted vases from the Middle Minoan period, rock crystal and carved, gilded vases, and ceramic cups in the shape of bulls' heads. A Daedalus-like ingenuity is shown in two finds from the 16th century B.C., a wine press built in carved-out layers of rock and a 17-inch-high stone pedestal designed to hold several different detachable table tops.

Critius (krish′i-us, krit′-) and **Nesiotes** (nes-i-ō′tēz, nē-shi-). Greek sculptors of the 5th century B.C. Critius is thought to have been a pupil of Antenor, creator of the famous statues of Harmodius and Aristogiton, which were carried off from Athens by Xerxes and later recovered. Meanwhile Critius and Nesiotes executed new figures to replace those taken away by the Persians. Two sculptures at Naples have been identified as copies of these works, one of which, however, has been restored with a head of 4th century workmanship. Very little is known about Nesiotes, but Critius had a school of sculpture at Athens and among his works was a statue of Apollo with the lyre.

Cupid (kū′pid) and **Psyche** (sī′kē). Copy in marble, in the Capitoline Museum, Rome, of a Greek original of Hellenistic date, representing a boy and a girl embrac-

fat, fāte, fär, fåll, åsk, fāre; net, mē, hèr; pin, pīne; not, nōte, möve, nôr; up, lūte, půll; oi, oil; ou out; (lightened) ēlect, agǫny, ūnite;

ing. Cupid is nude, Psyche draped from the hips down.

Cyathus (sī′a-thus). [Also: *Kyathos.*] In ancient Greece, a form of vase or cup with a long handle, used especially for dipping, as for taking wine from the crater to pour into the oinochoë or directly into the cup. It was often made in the form of a ladle.

——D——

Damophon (dam′ō-fon). Greek sculptor, born at Messene, Greece; fl. 2nd century B.C. He was one of the masters of Hellenistic art, and his work combines the decorative richness of his period with something of the monumental simplicity of the Phidian epoch. For a sanctuary of Demeter at Lycosura, in Arcadia, he designed a group of cult statues, of Demeter and Persephone, seated, flanked by standing figures of Artemis and the Titan Anytus, from which three heads and other fragments were recovered during excavations at the site. From the quality of the carving, scholars have speculated that the actual carving was done by apprentices from the master's clay models. Damophon is also credited with a statue of the Mother of the Gods for the agora of Messene, an acrolithic Ilithyia for Aegium, an Artemis, and many others. He worked also in gold and ivory, and it was he who restored the cracked ivory of Phidias' chryselephantine Zeus at Olympia. (JJ)

Deinocrates (dī-nok′ra-tēz). See *Dinocrates.*

Delos (dē′los). [Also: *Mikra Dilos;* ancient names, *Asteria, Ortygia.*] Smallest island of the Cyclades, Greece, situated in the narrow passage between the islands of Myconus and Rhenia. Area, two square miles. Here, according to some accounts, Asteria, daughter of the Titans Coeus and Phoebe, leaped into the sea to escape the embraces of Zeus and was transformed into a quail. A city was named Asteria for her, but afterward renamed Delos. Delos was also known, in her memory, as Ortygia, "quail." Leto, about to bear her children by Zeus, was pursued all over the world by a serpent sent to harass her by jealous Hera. As the time for her confinement neared, no place on earth would receive her out of fear of the anger of Hera. At last she came to Delos, at that time a floating island, and there she was welcomed and kindly received. Some say her children, Artemis and Apollo, were both born on the tiny island, but others say Artemis was born on neighboring Rhenia, and as soon as she was born, helped her mother across to Delos. The birth of Apollo took place in the shadow of the Hill of Cynthus, where the stream of the Inopus issues from the hill. The palm tree there, that Leto clasped when she bore Apollo, was one of the sights of antiquity from the time of Homer to that of Pliny. In its joy at being the birthplace of the god, the island covered itself with golden blossoms. Some say four pillars rose from the sea after the birth of the twin gods and moored the island, so that henceforth it ceased to float. Others say Apollo himself anchored the island, to reward it for receiving his mother. From earliest times, Delos was connected with the Hyperboreans. When Apollo and Artemis were born, some say, two Hyperborean maidens, Arge and Opis, came to Delos to help the birth goddess deliver the children of Leto. The Hyperborean damsels died on Delos and were entombed behind the temple of Artemis. Ever after they were honored by the Delian women from whom the rest of the islanders learned to honor them also. Later two more Hyperborean maidens, Hyperoche and Laodice, came to Delos, accompanied by several men. They brought offerings wrapped in wheaten straw. These maidens also died on Delos and were entombed. In their honor the maidens of Delos cut off a lock of their hair before their wedding day and laid it upon the graves of the Hyperborean damsels.

The youths also made offerings of their hair on their tombs. When the Hyperboreans saw that their envoys did not return, they ceased to send them to Delos. Instead they sent their offerings to Scythia, from where they were conveyed in relays to Delos.

Delos became the seat of a great sanctuary in honor of Apollo, one of the most famous religious foundations of antiquity. From the time of Solon, Athens sent an annual embassy to the Delian festival, in which the "tunic-trailing Ionians" honored Apollo with boxing, dancing, and song. When Pisistratus regained control of Athens for the third time (c544 or 541 B.C.), he purified Delos, on the advice of an oracle, by having all

MARBLE LION
Delos, 6th century B.C.
Greek National Tourist Office

the bodies that were buried within sight of the temple dug up and reburied in another part of the island. Only the tomb of the two Hyperborean maidens who came to assist at the birth of Apollo and Artemis were left untouched. This spot was sacred and was not disturbed. In the Persian War, Datis assembled the Persian fleet off Delos. The Delians fled from their island and refused to return, even though Datis assured them that he would do no harm to the land that was the birthplace of two gods. On the contrary, he landed and made an offering of 300 talents' weight of frankincense on the altar at Delos and then sailed away. After he left, Delos was shaken by an earthquake. This was the first time such a thing had occurred and was taken as a warning of evils to come to Greece, and as a fulfillment of the oracle that had predicted:

"Delos self will I shake, which never yet has been shaken."

But Datis himself so much respected the sacred place that on his way back to Asia, after Marathon, he stopped at Delos and left a golden image of Apollo that had been stolen by some of his Phoenician allies and hidden on their ship. He asked the Delians to return it to the temple from which it had been stolen. Twenty years later, in obedience to an oracle, the Delians did so.

After the Persian War, Delos was the center of the Delian League, formed (c477 B.C.) to resist Persian aggression. In 454 B.C. the sacred treasure of Delos, contributed by the members of the League, was removed to the Athenian Acropolis. In 426 B.C., Delos was purified again; all the dead who had been buried on the island were removed. Thenceforth no one was permitted to be born on the island, and no corpses could be buried there. The seriously ill were removed to some other place so as not to desecrate the island by dying there. Expectant mothers were taken off well before their time came so that no mortal children should first see the light of day in the island where Apollo was born. Games in honor of Apollo were restored, and a few years later all the inhabitants of the island were removed and it became purely a sacred place. The island was an Athenian dependency down to the Macedonian period, when it became semi-independent, and in the 2nd century B.C. it again became subject to Athens. The city of Delos was made a free port by the Romans and developed into a great commercial mart. It was raided in 88 B.C. by the forces of Mithridates VI and soon fell to the status of an almost uninhabited place. Now it is uninhabited. The sanctuary of Apollo was excavated by the French School at Athens, beginning in 1873. The work ranks as one of the chief achievements of its kind. The buildings disclosed lie for the most part within the enclosure or temenos of Apollo, which is of trapeziform shape, and about 650 feet to a side. Mosaic floors, bathing rooms, large underground drainage wells, and the floor plans of many buildings have been uncovered. In 1960 it was reported that ruins of a section of an ancient town had been discovered on the western slopes of the Hill of Cynthus. The finds there include the foundations of a large building with remains of a mosaic pavement worked in geometric designs. In addition to the interesting finds of architecture and sculpture, epigraphical discoveries of the highest importance have been made, bearing upon history and particularly upon the ceremonial and administration of the sanctuary.

Delphi (del'fi). [Also: **Delphoi.**] In ancient geography, a town in Phocis, Greece; the seat of the world-renowned oracle of Pythian Apollo, the most famous oracle of antiquity. It lies at an altitude of about 2000 feet, on the slopes of Mount Parnassus, whose peak rises to a height of more than 8000 feet to the NE. Towering 800 feet immediately above the sanctuary, on the N and E, are two great bare gray rocks, the Phaedriades or "shining ones." The Phaedriades are separated by a deep gorge at whose eastern foot is the sacred spring of Castalia. To the S, the ground falls

(obscured) errant, ardent, actor; ch, chip; g, go; th, thin; ᴛʜ, then; y, you; (variable) ḍ as d or j, ṣ as s or sh, ṭ as t or ch, ẓ as z or zh.

away swiftly to the ravine cut by the Plistus River as it flows into the Gulf of Corinth at the ancient port of Cirrha (Itea), six miles away. The area is subject to earthquakes and the menace of rock slides. Fissures opened up in the ground, and closed again by tremors, exhaled vapors said to inspire the priestesses who inhaled them to prophecy. In its location alone, Delphi is majestic and dramatic, the "wild and rocky glen" described by the poets.

From remote ages this was the seat of an oracle. Because it was subject to violent earthquakes, the earliest oracle belonged to the chthonian gods, those who hold sway under the earth. The most ancient oracle belonged to Gaea (Earth). Some say Poseidon, "the earth-shaker," shared the oracle with her. Through her prophetess Daphnis, a nymph of Mount Parnassus, Gaea gave her oracles. Poseidon uttered his through priests called Pyrcones. Gaea set the serpent Pytho to guard the chasm whence the prophetic vapors emanated. Her priestesses were called Pythia. Some say Gaea gave her share of the oracle to Themis, but Pytho continued to guard it. This was the situation until Apollo arrived, a relative newcomer to an ancient oracle. Some say he took the form of a dolphin (hence his epithet *Delphian Apollo*), and swam with a Cretan ship to the port of Cirrha. Arrived there, he resumed his divine form and commanded the Cretans to become his priests. When they protested that no one would come to worship at such a remote spot, he promised that so many would bring offerings that the sacrificial axes would never be idle. Having reassured them, he went to the chasm and slew the dragon that guarded the oracle. Some say the place was first named Pytho, "the place of the rotting," because he left the bones of the dragon to rot there, and that it was later named Delphi because Apollo had come to the nearby shores in the shape of a dolphin. But some say it was named Delphi in honor of Delphus, a son or a descendant of

fat, fāte, fär, fåll, åsk, fãre; net, mē, hėr; pin, pīne; not, nōte, möve, nôr; up, lūte, pùll; oi, oil; ou out; (lightened) ḝlect, agǫny, ūnite;

Johnson State College
Johnson, VT. 05656

Apollo. Apollo received Poseidon's share in the oracle in exchange for a place near Troezen, in the Peloponnesus, and became sole master at Delphi. Having killed Pytho, Apollo was compelled to seek purification, and was away doing penance for eight years. The penance and purification of Apollo were commemorated in a sacred drama that was enacted at Delphi, at first, every eight years. The epithet *Pythian* was given to Apollo because he slew the dragon; his priestesses were called Pythia, or sometimes, Pythonesses. Others say, and the two legends existed side by side, that Apollo came from the land of the Hyperboreans at the back of the north wind, and seized the oracle. These say that his first prophet, the only man who ever served in this capacity, was Olen, a Hyperborean. But most say that Phemenoë was his first prophetess, and that she pronounced her oracles in hexameter verse. At first the priestess was available for consultation only once a year, on Apollo's birthday. In later times she prophesied once a month, or every day, if the omens were favorable. Those who sought advice from the oracle came as suppliants, wearing laurel wreaths and fillets of wool; they purified themselves, sacrificed a victim, and inquired whether it was worth their while to ask a question. If the response to this query was favorable, they approached the priestess in her shrine. Three priestesses served in turn. The priestess was purified, drank the waters of the spring of Cassotis, chewed laurel leaves, and seated herself on a tripod over the chasm from which the vapors issued and which stimulated prophetic utterance. Only a priest was present when the priestess gave her responses. His function was to interpret the utterances, which were often obscure or, at the least, capable of two interpretations. Heracles, seeking information from the oracle, was denied by the priestess because of his impurity. Enraged, Heracles attempted to seize the sacred tripod and threatened to set up his own oracle. Apollo came to

(obscured) errạnt, ardẹnt, actǫr; ch, chip; g, go; th, thin; ŦH, then; y, you;
(variable) ḍ as d or j, ş as s or sh, ṭ as t or ch, ẓ as z or zh.

protect his shrine and the two struggled until Zeus parted them by a thunderbolt and forced them to compose their differences. The priestess gave Heracles a response, and the sanctuary remained firmly in Apollo's hands. Some say that the myth of the fight between Heracles and Apollo symbolizes the Dorian invasion of Greece (c1100 B.C.). Most of the Dorians went on into the Peloponnesus, but some remained in Doris and continued to have great influence over the sanctuary. After the Dorian invasion the influence and power of the sanctuary flourished, and in the succeeding period of more than a thousand years, was felt from the shores of Asia to Rome. Other gods came to share the sacred spot with Apollo. Athena Pronoea *(Forethought)* had her place. Her sanctuary was on a slope below the temple of Apollo. (The temples in her precinct fell into ruin and the spot became known as the *Marmaria*,

Tholos, Delphi
Greek National Tourist Office

roughly, "the marble quarry," from the many fragments there.) Dionysus, an oracular god who prophesied during the winter, when Apollo was off with the Hyperboreans, was consulted. He was considered a god who died and was reborn annually, and his tomb at Delphi was the scene of rites held by women. Delphi also possessed the "omphalos" *(navel)*, a stone that represented the exact center of the world. The myth was that Zeus sent out two eagles in opposite directions to make a circuit of the universe. They met at Delphi, and established it as the center. Another stone, or possibly it was the same one, was also called "omphalos," and was the stone given by Rhea to Cronus in place of her new-born son Zeus. A sacred city grew up around the oracle and these cult objects. According to tradition the first temple erected on the site was a hut of branches of laurel, a tree sacred to Apollo. This was replaced by a temple made by the bees, of beeswax and feathers, and sent to Delphi by the Hyperboreans. The third temple was of wood, covered with bronze plates and was made, some say, by Hephaestus. Of these three temples no trace has ever been found. The fourth temple was of stone. Trophonius and Agamedes, according to tradition, were the builders.

Delphi was at first under the control of Crissa, in Phocis, whose territory included the port of Cirrha. Pilgrims, making their way to the sanctuary, were subject to all sorts of dues and exactions by the Crissaeans. The priests of Delphi complained to the Amphictyonic Council, a group of representatives from 12 Greek cities (mostly Thessalian and Dorian), that had its seat at Anthela. The members were pledged to aid each other. The Amphictyons acted against Crissa. Solon of Athens and Clisthenes, tyrant of Sicyon, lent their assistance in the Sacred War (c600–c590 B.C.). Crissa was destroyed, its territory was dedicated to Apollo and henceforth the tilling of the Crissaean plain was forbidden, and Delphi became autonomous. The man-

agement of the sanctuary was left in the hands of the
Amphictyonic Council. The Pythian Games, de-
scended from the old religious drama representing the
purification of Apollo (the *Stepteria*), and with the addition of musical and athletic contests, also came under
the supervision of the Council. Thereafter, from 586
B.C., the Games were held every four years. The end
of the Sacred War marked the beginning of a period

SPHINX, C550 B.C.
Delphi

of great prosperity for Delphi. The treasuries of Corinth and Sicyon were dedicated. Cypselus, tyrant of
Corinth (c655–625 B.C.), was said to have dedicated
the former, and Clisthenes the latter. These treasuries,
the earliest of many, were small temple-like structures
erected and dedicated by individual city-states. In
them sacred, and often precious, vessels for religious

ceremonies were kept. Rich offerings were made to them, and they also served as meeting places for pilgrims and officials from the cities that had dedicated them. The Lydian kings, Gyges (c685–653 B.C.), and Croesus (6th century king who reigned from 560–546 B.C.), made rich gifts to the sanctuary in gratitude for favorable oracles. Amasis II (fl. c569–525 B.C.), of Egypt was also a contributor. In 548 B.C. the temple built by Trophonius and Agamedes was destroyed by fire. The Alcmaeonidae, aristocrats who had been exiled from Athens, raised a great sum to rebuild it. Croesus and Amasis II again made large contributions for this cause. Spintharus of Corinth was the architect. At their own expense, it was said, the Alcmaeonidae had the temple faced with Parian marble instead of the limestone that was called for by the plan. The treasury of the Siphnians, one of the richest of them all, was

BATTLE OF THE GODS AND GIANTS
From the N frieze of the Siphnian Treasury, c525 B.C.
Delphi

(obscured) errạnt, ardẹnt, actọr; ch, chip; g, go; th, thin; ᴛʜ, then; y, you; (variable) ḍ as d or j, ṣ as s or sh, ṭ as t or ch, ẓ as z or zh.

dedicated c524 B.C. (Large fragments of its pediments
and friezes, depicting the Greeks and the Trojans in
combat, War of the Giants, the Judgment of Paris, and
the exploits of Heracles, are preserved in the museum
at Delphi.) Toward the close of the 6th century, the
Athenians dedicated the Treasury of Athens at Delphi,

Athenian Treasury, Delphi, c490 B.C.
Greek National Tourist Office

perhaps to celebrate the overthrow (507 B.C.) of the
aristocratic party at Athens and the success of the dem-
ocratic party of Clisthenes. The walls of their treasury
were covered with inscriptions, many of which record

the gratitude of freed slaves. Among the inscriptions is also a hymn to Apollo bearing the only recorded musical notations ever found in Greece. (The rebuilt treasury of Athens is one of the sights of Delphi. The fitting together of the scattered and broken walls, tumbled down and fragmented by earthquakes, was greatly facilitated by matching the inscriptions.) The Cnidians raised their *Lesche,* a kind of club house, in the first half of the 5th century B.C. Its walls were decorated with paintings by the Thasian artist Polygnotus.

Croesus, who had made such rich gifts to Delphi in return for favorable responses, was later one of the most ill-fated victims of its obscure pronouncements. Having made every provision to secure the most reliable oracle, he sent to Delphi to ask if he should wage war on Cyrus. He learned that if he crossed the Halys River and marched against the Persians, he would destroy a great empire. Greatly encouraged, he attacked Cyrus and destroyed a great empire—his own. When he reproached the priestess, he was told that he had misinterpreted ' the oracle, which had been duly fulfilled. Croesus humbly acknowledged his error, so it is said. Not all the answers, however, were equivocal. In a later time the question was put: who was the wisest man in the world? The priestess replied with the flat statement that there was no man in the world wiser than Socrates.

When the Persians invaded Europe in 490 B.C., Delphi feared to be destroyed if it resisted, and "medized," that is, it was favorable to the Persians. But the priests were able to gloss over this period of weakness. Ten years after Marathon the Persians returned. When Xerxes had taken the pass at Thermopylae, he sent an army into Phocis to plunder the sanctuary of Delphi, of whose treasures, according to Herodotus, he knew more than those in his own palace; he had heard so much about them. The Delphians were stricken with terror and asked the oracle if they should bury the

(obscured) errạnt, ardẹnt, actọr; ch, chip; g, go; th, thin; ᴛʜ, then; y, you; (variable) ḏ as d or j, ṣ as s or sh, ṯ as t or ch, ẕ as z or zh.

treasures or remove them to another place. The god replied, through his priestess, that he was well able without their help to protect his own. On receiving the response the Delphians concentrated on saving themselves and their goods. They retired, some across the Gulf of Corinth and some to the heights of Parnassus. Only 60 men and a prophet remained in the sanctuary. When the Persians approached, the prophet saw the sacred armor divinely removed from the shrine. The Persians advanced to the shrine of Athena Pronoea. Suddenly there was a crack of thunder. Two immense crags split off from Mount Parnassus and rolled down on the Persians, crushing a great number of them, while from the temple of Athena were heard a war-cry and a shout of victory. The Persians, terrified by the portents, fled in confusion. The Delphians, seeing how the god protected his own, fell on the Persians and slaughtered them wholesale. Those who escaped were pursued into Boeotia by two gigantic armed warriors, heroes who had sacred precincts at Delphi. Herodotus, who tells this tale, saw the huge stones that had crushed the Persians in the precinct of Athena Pronoea. Before this miraculous event, the Athenians had sent envoys to consult the oracle as to their defense against the Persians. The priestess replied:

"Wretches, why sit ye here? Fly, fly to the ends of creation,
Quitting your homes, and the crags which your city crowns with her circlet.
All—all ruined and lost. Since fire, and impetuous Ares,
Speeding along in a Syrian chariot, hastes to destroy her."

The envoys refused to return to Athens with such a gloomy reply. They returned to the shrine as suppliants and vowed to die in the sanctuary rather than leave without some more encouraging word. It would be the greatest impiety if any died in the shrine. The

fat, fāte, fär, fåll, àsk, fãre; net, mē, hėr; pin, pīne; not, nōte, mŏve, nôr; up, lūte, pùll; oi, oil; ou out; (lightened) ĕlect, agǫny, ūnite;

priestess grudgingly and obscurely uttered the following:

"Safe shall the wooden wall continue for thee and thy children."

Themistocles interpreted the "wooden wall" to mean the fleet, worked to build it up, and went on to defeat the Persians at Salamis. The temporizing of Delphi was forgotten when the Persians were driven out. Rich offerings of trophies, statues, and tripods were made for the victories of Salamis, Plataea, and Mycale. The offering for Plataea was a golden tripod set upon a pillar of three bronze intertwined serpents. On its base were inscribed the names of the Greek peoples who dedicated it.

Following the Persian War, Delphi became embroiled in the disputes between the various city-states, and lost some of its credit, because it seemed to take sides and because the charge of bribery leveled against it was never satisfactorily cleared. In the Second Sacred War (c448 B.C.), Pericles returned control of Delphi to the Phocians, but it regained its autonomy by the Peace of Nicias (421 B.C.), according to the terms of which the common temples of Greece were to be free to all. As a great sanctuary, it continued to receive gifts and offerings from the rival city-states and from foreign rulers as well. In 373 B.C. the temple was destroyed by an earthquake. Funds were raised by international subscription, and construction of a new temple was begun which was finished c330 B.C. Before its completion, a Third Sacred War broke out (357–346 B.C.) when the Phocians cultivated the sacred plain of Crissa and were punished by the Amphictyonic Council. Philomelus, the Phocian general, pillaged the rich treasures of the sanctuary to build a fortress. Philip of Macedon intervened, crushed the Phocians and imposed a heavy fine on them. Peace was short-lived. The city of Amphissa committed impiety against Delphi (339 B.C.), and brought on the Fourth Sacred

War. Philip of Macedon, who had taken the place of the Phocians in the Amphictyonic League, interfered to "restore order." The Athenians and Thebans, fearing his growing power in Greece, resisted him, and he overwhelmingly defeated them at Chaeronea, 338 B.C. In 279 B.C., the Gauls, under Brennus, attacked Delphi and were driven off, so it was said, by the direct inter-

Temple of Apollo, Delphi, c330 B.C.
Greek National Tourist Office

vention of the god, who sent earthquakes, snow, and bitter cold to repulse them. After 189 B.C., Delphi came under the dominion of the Romans. In 91 B.C.

fat, fāte, fär, fåll, åsk, fāre; net, mē, hèr; pin, pīne; not, nōte, möve, nôr; up, lūte, pùll; oi, oil; ou out; (lightened) ĕlect, agŏny, ūnite;

Standing female figure
with pomegranate
Marble, early 6th century B.C.

The Metropolitan Museum of Art

Youth of the Apollo type
Athenian, marble
615–600 B.C.

Staatliche Museen, Berlin

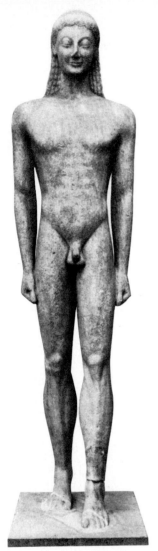

Tombstone of Aristion
Marble
Late 6th century B.C.

*National Museum
Athens*

Standing Youth
Melos, marble
c560 B.C.

*National Museum
Athens*

National Museum, Athens

Four youths in starting positions
for various athletic exercises
Marble relief
Late 6th century B.C.

The Youth Kroisos
Marble, c520 B.C.

*National Museum
Athens*

Delphi

The Charioteer
Bronze, c470 B.C.

Museo delle Terme, Rome

Museum of Fine Arts, Boston

Female flute player
Side panel from the so-called
Ludovisi throne, marble, c460 B.C.

Boy with lyre
Detail from three-sided relief
Marble, 470–460 B.C.

Louvre

Head of Apollo of Piombino
Bronze, c475 B.C.

Acropolis Museum

Votive relief of Athena
Marble, before the
mid-5th century B.C.

National Museum, Athens

Poseidon
Found in the sea off Cape Artemisium
Bronze, shortly before mid-5th century B.C.

Standing Youth
Detail

Standing Youth
Found in the sea
off Marathon
Bronze, 350–325 B.C

National Museum, Athens

National Museum, Athens

Sepulchral Stele for a Youth
Salamis, marble, c420 B.C.

Head of an African
Cyrene, bronze, first
half of the 4th
century B.C.

British Museum

Head of a Boxer
Olympia, bronze
Late 4th century B.C.

National Museum, Athens

British Museum

Sculptured base of column from the later temple
of Artemis at Ephesus, marble, c340 B.C.

Antikensammlungen
Munich

Bronze statuette
Beroea, c400 B.C.

Standing Woman
Terra-cotta figurine
4th century B.C.

The Metropolitan Museum of Art

Museum of Fine Arts, Boston

Head of a Young Goddess
Chios, marble, c300 B.C.

Staatliche Museen, Berlin

Aphrodite
Terra-cotta statuette
End of 2nd century B.C.

Museum Antiker Kleinkunst
Munich

Attic Geometric amphora
Mid-8th century B.C.

Protoattic amphora
7th century B.C.

Louvre

National Museum, Athens

Neck amphora, 7th century B.C.
Neck: Heracles Slaying Nessus; body: Gorgons

British Museum

Louvre

Corinthian wine-jug,
625–600 B.C.

Early Corinthian alabastron,
625–600 B.C.

Staatliche Museen, Berlin

Middle Corinthian aryballus
Griffin, early 6th century B.C.

Louvre

Corinthian crater
Heracles Feasting with Eurytus, end of 7th century B.C.

Louvre

Attic black-figured dinos
Death of Medusa, c600–590 B.C.

Museo Archeologico, Florence

Cleitias, François Vase, c570 B.C.
Neck: Calydonian Boar Hunt
Funeral Games for Patroclus
Body: Wedding of Peleus and Thetis
Achilles Pursuing Troilus
Real and Fabulous Animals
Foot: Battle of Cranes and Pygmies

Bibliothèque Nationale, Paris

Arcesilaus Painter, Laconian cup
King Arcesilaus Supervising the Weighing of Silphion, c565–560 B.C.

Louvre

Black-figured hydria
Hermes Stealing Apollo's Cattle
Mid-6th century B.C.

Chalcidian crater
Two Youths Preparing
To Go Riding, 550–530 B.C.

British Museum

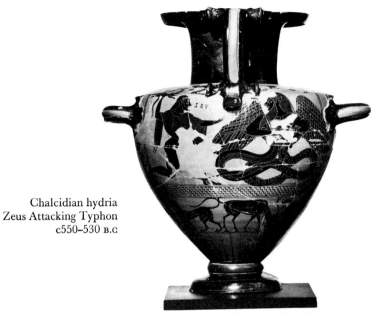

Chalcidian hydria
Zeus Attacking Typhon
c550–530 B.C

Museum Antiker Kleinkunst, Munich

Amasis Painter
Neck amphora
Dionysus and Maenads, c540 B.C.

Bibliothèque Nationale, Paris

Museum Antiker Kleinkunst
Munich

Exekias
Cup interior, Dionysus in a Boat, c535 B.C.

British Museum

Tleson Painter
Signed cup interior, Hunter,
3rd quarter of 6th century B.C.

Panathenaic Prize amphora
c530 B.C.

The Metropolitan Museum of Art

British Museum

Exekias
Attic black-figured amphora, c540–530 B.C.
Achilles Killing Penthesilea

Museo Nazionale, Tarquinia

Oltos
Cup, Gods in Olympus, c530–510 B.C.

Antikensammlungen, Munich

Phintias
Red–figured kylix, c520 B.C.
(A) Heracles and Apollo Struggling for the Tripod; (B) Heracles
Slaying Alcyoneus, in the Presence of Hermes; (C) Side view

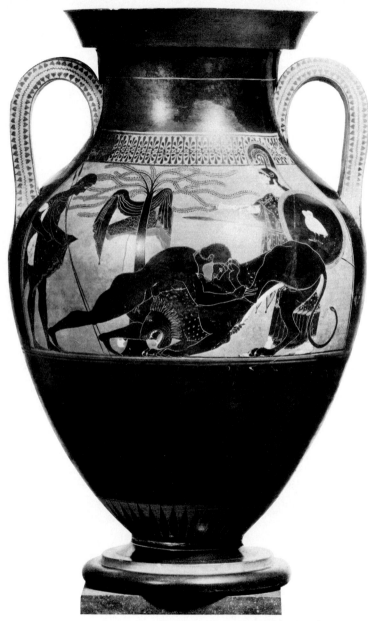

Museo Civico, Brescia

Psiax
Black-figured amphora, c520 B.C.
Heracles and the Nemean Lion

British Museum

Attic black–figured amphora, c510 B.C.
Heracles Delivering the Erymanthian Boar to Eurystheus

Black-figured (white ground) Attic lecythus
Poseidon Fishing, c515 B.C.

The Metropolitan Museum of Art

Louvre

Museum Antiker Kleinkunst
Munich

Andocides Painter
Red-figured amphora, c510 B.C.
Heracles and Cerberus

Red-figured amphora, c510 B.C.
Male Revelers

Phintias
Red-figured hydria,
c510 B.C.
The Music Lesson

Antikensammlungen, Munich

Louvre

Euphronius
Signed red-figured crater, end of 6th century B.C.
Combat of Heracles and Antaeus

Myson
Red-figured amphora
c500 B.C.
Croesus on His Pyre

Louvre

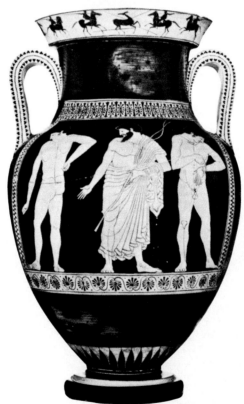

Antikensammlungen, Munich

Cleophrades Painter
Red-figured amphora, c500 B.C.
Lid: Chariot Race; amphora: Athletes

Antikensammlungen, Munich

Berlin Painter
Red-figured stamnos, c490 B.C.
Athena with Warriors

Antikensammlungen, Munich

Pan Painter
Red-figured psykter, c490 B.C.
Artemis between Apollo
and Evenus

British Museum

Attic red-figured cup
Medallion, 490–480 B.C.
Departing Warrior

*Museum Antiker Kleinkunst
Munich*

Brygos Painter
Medallion, cup interior
Maenad, c490 B.C.

British Museum

Pistoxenus Painter
White ground cup, 460 B.C.
Aphrodite Riding on a Goose

*Musées Royaux
d'Art et d'Histoire*

Duris
Kantharus, Heracles and the Amazons, 490–480 B.C.

the temple was burned by Thracians. In 86 B.C. Sulla pillaged the sanctuary. The story is that the priests, to deter Sulla from his purpose, set a harpist to playing in a concealed place and warned Sulla that the god was playing to forbid him to violate his temple. Sulla turned their remark by saying that the god was playing to show that he welcomed a friend, and proceeded to carry off what he wished. Later, the Emperor Nero carried off over 500 statues from the sacred city, but 3000 or so were still left there. Even so, Delphi retained great wealth. But it had lost its place as the center of the universe, and enjoyed only a short revival as a religious center under Hadrian. In the reigns of Constantine and Theodosius many of its treasures were stolen to adorn other capitals, including the golden tripod of Plataea, which Constantine set up in the city named for him. Theodosius II, a Christian emperor, delivered the final blow to Delphi when he silenced the oracle, destroyed (390 A.D.) the temple, and systematically mutilated the statues and images.

The influence of Delphi was felt throughout the Mediterranean world for a period of centuries. It received pilgrims and envoys from all quarters, and became a great clearing house for receiving and spreading information. No colonizing force set out from Greece before consulting the oracle. Political decisions were based on its responses. It was the arbiter in education, art, and literature, as well as in religion. It was an enlightening and elevating force, emphasizing as it did on many occasions, a rule of law rather than of vengeance, moral purity rather than purifying rites. With the Pythian Games it brought the Greeks together, in athletics, musical contests, and literary competitions, and stressed the tendencies that unified the Greeks rather than those which divided them. In addition, as the recipient of rich gifts from city-states, generals, heroes, kings, victors in athletic contests, grateful individuals, and even beautiful women, Delphi was the art center of Greece. Images and statues by the finest sculptors over the course of centuries adorned the sanctuary and its environs. Among them was the famous bronze *Charioteer* on view in the museum at Delphi today. The site was occupied by a great temple of Apollo, to which pilgrims ascended by a winding sacred way that was lined with treasuries and votive offerings. All around the temple were other shrines and buildings, as well as uncounted hundreds of statues. In the flanks of the hill that rises sharply behind Apollo's temple was a theater, near the fountain of Cassotis whose waters flowed underground into the shrine and were drunk by the priestesses. Above the theater was a stadium where certain of the contests were held. The stadium, remains of which can still be seen, replaced an earlier one on the plain around Crissa. The sacred monuments and temples were carried off or destroyed, early in the Christian era. Earthquakes and landslides covered the site. A village, Castri, grew up over the buried remains. In 1892, the entire village having been removed to a new site, French excavators began work there. In succeeding years, many remains of the ancient site have been uncovered, including the temple of Apollo, the theater, bases of votive offerings and sites of treasuries, so that today it is possible not only to admire the imposing majesty of the physical scene, but to recreate, with the help of some imagination, the profusion and richness of the site as it existed in an earlier time.

Demeter of Cnidus (dḗ-mē′tẽr; nī′dus). Greek statue (4th century B.C.) of the school of Scopas, now in the British Museum at London. The goddess is represented, fully draped and seated, as mourning for her daughter, and conveys a feeling of profound grief.

Dexileus (dek-sil′ḗ-us), **Monument of.** Monument on the Street of Tombs at Athens. It is a beautiful stele bearing in relief a youthful horseman who has ridden down

fat, fāte, fär, fâll, ȧsk, fãre; net, mē, hẽr; pin, pīne; not, nōte, mȯve, nôr; up, lūte, pull; oi, oil; ou out; (lightened) ḙlect, agǫny, ṳnite;

an enemy. Dexileus fell before Corinth in 394 or 393 B.C.

TOMBSTONE OF DEXILEUS
Ceramicus Museum, Athens
T.A.P. Service

(obscured) errạnt, ardẹnt, actọr; ch, chip; g, go; th, thin; ŦH, then; y, you;
(variable) ḍ as d or j, ṣ as s or sh, ṭ as t or ch, ẓ as z or zh.

Diadumenos (dī-a̤-dū′me̤-nos). Athlete binding his brow with a fillet, by the 5th century Greek sculptor Polyclitus, known from a Hellenistic copy found at Delos, now in Athens, and a head in Dresden. (JJ)

Diana of Versailles (dī-an′a̤; ver-sālz′, ver-sī′). [Also: **Diana the Huntress**.] Greek statue in the Louvre, Paris, commonly regarded as a companion piece to the *Apollo Belvedere*, though inferior in execution. The goddess is advancing, clad in the short Dorian tunic and himation girded at her waist; she looks toward the right, as with raised arm she takes an arrow from her quiver.

Dibutades (dī-bū′ta̤-dēz). Greek sculptor of Sicyon, the reputed inventor of relief sculpture.

Didymaeum (did-i-mē′um). A temple or shrine sacred to Zeus and Apollo at Didyma or Branchidae near Miletus. There was a sacred way leading to it which had been built for an earlier temple on the site, and which was bordered by a series of archaic seated figures. The later building probably dates from about 334 B.C. It was dipteral, with the cella open to the sky.

Dinocrates or **Deinocrates** (dī-nok′ra̤-tēz). Ablest of the architects of Alexander the Great; fl. 4th century B.C. He planned the new city of Alexandria, and rebuilt the Artemisium of Ephesus after its destruction by fire. He had a plan, never executed, of making a huge statue of a seated figure of Mount Athos (the mountain, personified, was to have a city in one hand and a basin to catch the rivers in the other).

Dipoenus and **Scyllis** (dī-pē′nus; sil′is). Greek sculptors of the archaic period (fl. c580 B.C.). They worked together and their names are always coupled. They executed sculptures in wood and ivory and also, it is thought, in marble. Some say they were sons or pupils of Daedalus, and that Scyllis invented the art of carving in marble. Little is really known about them, although Pliny the Elder mentions that they worked at Sicyon, and it is thought that the noted school of sculpture at that city owed its rise to them.

Dipteral (dip′tẹ-rạl). In architecture, consisting of or furnished with a double row of columns. A dipteral temple is one in which the cella is entirely surrounded by a double row of columns.

Dipylon Gate (dip′i-lon). Chief gateway of ancient Athens, traversing the walls on the NW side. As its name indicates, it was in fact a double gate, consisting of a strongly fortified rectangular court between an outer and an inner portal. Each portal also was double, having two doors, each 11⅓ feet wide, separated by a central pier. The foundations of this gate, alone among those of ancient Athens, survive in great part, and from it toward the SW extends a beautiful stretch of the original wall of Themistocles, built under Peloponnesian menace after the Greek victories over the Persians in 480 and 479 B.C. This wall, in its contrasted construction of admirably fitted blocks and rough stones, confirms literary witness to the haste of work spurred on by emergency. The Dipylon is identical with the Sacred Gate, and among the roads diverging from it is the Sacred Way to Eleusis. It was long held that an opening in the wall immediately SW of the Dipylon was the Sacred Gate, but Dörpfeld found that this was a passage for the stream which he identified as the Eridanus.

Discobolus (dis-kob′ọ-lus). Statue of a discus thrower by Myron, Greek sculptor of the 5th century B.C., known from literary descriptions and from copies in Rome (the Lancalotti head, the torso in the Museo Nazionale, the Vatican restoration) and in the British Museum. The body is bent forward and turned toward the right as the heavy discus is swung back, wonderful art being shown in the choice and expression of the moment of repose when, the backward motion completed, the powerful cast forward is on the point of execution.

Doric Order (dor′ik). In architecture, the oldest and strongest of the three Greek orders, in its external forms the simplest of all, but in its most perfect exam-

(obscured) errạnt, ardẹnt, actọr; ch, chip; g, go; th, thin; ŦH, then; y, you; (variable) ḍ as d or j, ṣ as s or sh, ṭ as t or ch, ẓ as z or zh.

ples, especially as exhibited in the monuments of the age of Pericles at Athens, combining with solidity and force the most subtle and delicate refinement of outlines and proportions that architecture has known. A characteristic of the Grecian Doric column is the ab-

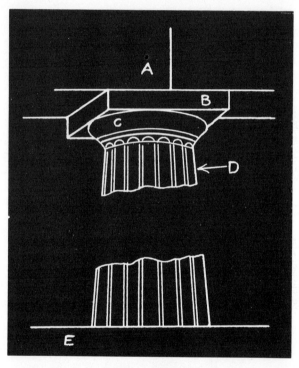

DORIC ORDER
A) architrave; B) abacus; C) echinus; D) shaft; E) stylobate

sence of a base; the channelings are usually 20 in number, and in section approximate to a semi-ellipse; the capital has generally no astragal (an ornamental molding), but only one or more fillets or annulets, which separate the channelings from the echinus (convex projecting molding of eccentric curve, supporting the abacus). The profile of the capital in the best examples is a carefully studied eccentric curve, neither flat enough to be hard in effect, nor full enough to be weak. The echinus prior to the time of perfection spread out far beyond the shaft; the later Greeks made it a frustum of a cone. In good Greek examples, as a rule, no horizontal lines are found in a Doric building, floor- and cornice-lines, etc., being curved slightly upward, the profiles of the column-shafts are slightly convex, and all columns are slightly inclined toward the center of the building. All these particularities have relation to the optical effects so subtle that their influence is felt rather than seen.

Doryphorus (do̅-rif'o̅-rus). In Greek antiquity, and in art and archaeology, a spear-bearer, a man armed with a spear; specifically, a nude figure, or one almost nude, holding a spear or lance: a favorite subject with ancient sculptors. The most noted Doryphorus was that by the great artist Polyclitus, best known from the copy in Naples, which is regarded as his celebrated canon or

DURIS
Athena with Heracles, red-figured cup, c480 B.C.
Munich

type of what the perfectly proportioned human figure should be.

Duris (dū′ris). Attic potter and painter in the red-figure style, active c500–470 B.C., fond of scenes from everyday life. Thirty vessels with his signature as painter are extant, and over 200 more have been attributed to him. Among his extant works is a kylix (Louvre) with Eos carrying off the body of her son Memnon, and a psykter (British Museum) with Satyrs. The inside of a cup (Munich) c480 B.C., shows Heracles resting as Athena pours wine into his cup. Scenes showing Peleus carrying off Thetis as her sisters run to their father for aid decorate the outside of the cup. This vessel was signed by Hieron as the potter. Another cup (Munich) shows a banqueter and a flute player on the inside, and Heracles striking his teacher Linus on the outside.

Dying Alexander (al-eg-zan′dèr). Name given to a sculptured head, held to be a Greek original of Hellenistic date, very remarkable for the intensity of its expression of pain, and of admirable execution.

Dying Gaul (gôl), **The**. [Formerly called **The Dying Gladiator**.] Ancient statue of the Pergamene school, in the Capitoline Museum, Rome. The warrior, nude, sits on the ground with bowed head, supporting himself with his right arm. The statue is considered especially fine in the mastery of anatomy displayed, and in its characterization of the racial type. It is thought possibly to have been commissioned by Attalus as a monument to his victories over the Gauls.

E

Echinus (e-kī'nus). In architecture, the convex projecting molding of eccentric curve supporting the abacus of the Doric capital; the corresponding feature in capitals of other orders.

Eleusis (ē̆-lö'sis). A little town about 14 miles W of Athens, in Attica, situated near the bay and opposite the island of Salamis. Eleusis *(Advent)* was one of the oldest of the parishes of Attica, the seat of a very ancient cult of Demeter, and of the famous Eleusinian mysteries. It was annexed to Athens in the 7th century B.C., but kept control of the mysteries, in the celebration of which the Athenians, as well as Greeks from all other states, annually came for initiation into and celebration of the rites. The observation of the mysteries of Demeter and Kore (Persephone) continued down to the end of the 4th century A.D. Politically, Eleusis played no role in the development of Greece, but its religious significance was of paramount importance. The most important monuments lay within the sacred enclosure at Eleusis, which consisted of a spacious terrace on the E slope of an acropolis, surrounded by a massive wall and towers. The earliest sanctuary antedated the 7th century B.C., and was reconstructed and enlarged in the 6th century B.C. by the Pisistratidae. In succeeding years it was further enlarged as the importance of the mysteries increased. During the Persian Wars it was burned, but was restored by Cimon and Pericles. Entrance to the sanctuary of the Great Goddesses (Demeter and Kore) was forbidden, on pain of death, to the uninitiated. Those who had been initiated, like the traveler Pausanias, never described the buildings within the wall, only ruins of which now remain. Before the sacred enclosure was a large paved court, constructed in Roman times, and nearby an ancient spring where pilgrims purified themselves. Also in the area was a large altar and a ditch where victims, sacrifices to the gods of the Underworld, were burned. A sacred way led to the sanctuary. On the right of the sacred way a grotto cut into the flank of the hill was the precinct of Pluto and represented the entrance to the Underworld by which Hades (Pluto) carried off Persephone. The sacred precinct was entered through two propylaea (of Roman construction) in succession, and its chief building was the Telesterion, where the rites of initiation took place, rites surrounded by a secrecy that was never entirely violated. The remains of the Telesterion date from the 6th century B.C., with additions made in the time of the Roman emperors, and replace much earlier buildings. The Telesterion was a huge, nearly square, roofed hall, on the four sides of which rows of seats, some of which were cut into the rock, were constructed for the *mystae* (initiated), who sat on them and observed the rites of initiation as they took place. The seats accommodated about 3000 spectators. The unique architecture of the Telesterion and its successive transformations, as well as remains of the entire precinct, were revealed by the excavations of the Archaeological Society of Athens and others, carried out at intervals since 1882.

Eleusis, Bas-relief of. Ancient Greek work of high artistic importance in the National Museum, Athens. It represents Demeter, Kore, and Triptolemus, and is most delicate in execution and expression. It dates from the early 5th century B.C.

Elgin Marbles (el'gin). Collection of Greek sculptures comprising the bulk of the surviving plastic decoration of the Parthenon, and a caryatid and column from the Erechtheum, and recognized as containing the finest existing productions of Greek sculpture. The marbles,

fat, fāte, fär, fåll, àsk, fāre; net, mē, hèr; pin, pīne; not, nōte, möve, nôr; up, lūte, pùll; oi, oil; ou out; (lightened) ēlect, agǫny, ūnite;

BAS-RELIEF OF ELEUSIS, C440 B.C.
National Museum, Athens
T.A.P. Service

now in the British Museum, were brought from Athens between 1801 and 1803 by Thomas Bruce, the 7th Earl of Elgin. The Parthenon sculptures were executed under the direction of Phidias, c440 B.C. The collection includes remains of the pediment statues in the round, a great part of the frieze, in low relief, about 525 ft. long, which surrounded the exterior of the cella, and 15 of the metopes of the exterior frieze, carved in very high relief with episodes of the contest between the Centaurs and the Lapiths. Among the chief of the pediment figures are the reclining figure of Theseus, Iris with wind-blown drapery, and the group of one reclining and two seated female figures popularly called the "Three Fates."

Endoeus (en-dē′us). Ionian sculptor, active in the latter part of the 6th century B.C. Some say he was a pupil of Daedalus and fled with him to Crete. Among his works, in the archaic style, was a statue of seated Athena on the Acropolis, and an ancient image of Athena at Tegea. He also made images for temples in Ionia, including an image of Artemis at Ephesus.

Endymion (en-dim′i-ọn), *Sleeping.* Classical statue in Parian marble, found in Hadrian's villa at Tivoli, Italy, and acquired by the National Museum at Stockholm, Sweden.

Entablature (en-tab′la̲-tu̲r). In architecture, the horizontal members of a lintel construction that rest on columns and extend upward to the pediment or to the roof; such horizontal members are the architrave, frieze, and cornice.

Epictetus (ep-ik-tē′tus). Attic potter and painter, active at the end of the 6th century B.C. His signature appears as potter on at least one vessel, and as painter on thirty vessels. He was one of the greatest masters of his time. About 80 of his works—mostly cups and plates—are extant. He worked in the red-figure style mainly, although in his early work he sometimes used the black-figure technique. A plate (British Museum) shows an

fat, fāte, fär, fâll, àsk, fāre; net, mē, hėr; pin, pīne; not, nōte, mȯve, nôr; up, lūte, pu̇ll; oi, oil; ou out; (lightened) ẹlect, agǫny, ụnite;

Leto and Aphrodite in the Lap of Peitho or Dione, from the E
pediment of the Parthenon
British Museum

(obscured) errạnt, ardẹnt, actọr; ch, chip; g, go; th, thin; ᵺ, then; y, you;
(variable) ḍ as d or j, ṣ as s or sh, ṭ as t or ch, ẓ as z or zh.

archer, possibly an Amazon. Another shows a satyr holding a wineskin.

Epidaurus (ep-i-dô′rus). Ancient town on the E coast of the Peloponnesus, in the district called Argolis. The land was especially sacred to Asclepius, for the Epidaurians said that when Phlegyas, the Lapith king, came to the Peloponnesus to spy out the land and learn whether its people were warlike, he brought his daughter Coronis with him, unaware that she was about to bear Apollo's child. When her child, Asclepius, was born, she exposed him on a mountain, formerly called Myrtium but subsequently named Nipple. A she-goat pastured on the mountain slopes nursed him, and the watch-dog of the flock stood guard over him. The shepherd of the flock remarked that one she-goat and the watch-dog were missing. He looked about for them and found them behind a bush, guarding an infant. As he approached to take up the infant, lightning flashed from the child's body. The shepherd concluded that it was a divine child and so left it to divine protection. From the beginning Asclepius was a god, and his fame as a healer spread throughout the land. The most famous of his sanctuaries had their origin in Epidaurus. Throughout the flourishing period of Greek history Epidaurus was an independent state, possessing a small territory, bounded on the W by Argeia, on the N by Corinthia, on the S by Troezenia, and on the E by the Saronic Gulf. It was the most celebrated seat of the ancient cult of Asclepius. The sanctuary occupied a valley among hills, at some distance from the city. The sacred grove was enclosed and contained a temple of Asclepius, in which lived tame sacred serpents, the architecturally important *tholos* (round building) of Polyclitus, extensive porticoes which served as hospitals to the sick who came to seek the aid of the god and his priests, and many votive offerings. As at Delos, no birth or death could take place in the sacred enclosure, and all offer-

fat, fāte, fär, fåll, åsk, fāre; net, mē, hėr; pin, pīne; not, nōte, mȯve, nôr; up, lūte, pu̇ll; oi, oil; ou out; (lightened) ĕlect, agǫny, ụnite;

ings must be consumed within it. In the temple was an ivory and gold image of the god, representing him seated, holding a staff in one hand, and the other hand held above the head of a serpent. A dog stretched out at the side of the image. Originally, suppliants at the temple slept in the open air, but in the time of the Romans shelters were built for them. On slabs about the precinct were inscribed the names of the people who had been cured by Asclepius and the diseases from which he had freed them. Pausanias tells of a very old slab on which it was recorded that Hippolytus dedicated 20 horses to the god, because Asclepius had

Theater at Epidaurus
Greek National Tourist Office

raised him from the dead. Outside of the sacred enclosure were the stadium, a gymnasium, propylaea, and other buildings, the arrangements for the collection and distribution of water being especially noteworthy. The theater at Epidaurus built probably by Polyclitus the Younger, was, and still is, unrivaled in its acoustical perfection. Extensive excavations conducted by the Archaeological Society of Athens (1881, *et seq.*) have greatly added to our knowledge of the sanctuary of Epidaurus.

Epinaos (ep-i-nā′os). An open vestibule behind the cella of some temples, corresponding to the pronaos in front.

Erechtheum (ẹ-rek′thẹ-um). The popular name of a white marble temple of Athena, of the Ionic order, on the Acropolis of Athens, dating from the last quarter of the 5th century B.C. and one of the most remarkable creations of Greek architecture. In plan it is unique; whereas at this period Greek temples were almost invariably peristyle (surrounded by colonnades) or amphiprostyle (columned porches on front and rear), the

Erechtheum
Lillian Travis

Erechtheum has a conventional hexastyle porch on the E, but at the W, where the still more ancient sanctuary of Cecrops resisted encroachment, there are no steps and no free-standing columns, the order of the E front being suggested by four attached Ionic half-columns between antae, rising above a high basement. At the W end of the N flank is a deep porch, four columns in front and one behind each corner column, leading to the magnificent North Doorway which gave access to the W chambers. At the W end of the S flank is a porch ("Porch of the Maidens") in which six architectural statues of fully-draped young women ("Caryatids") take the place of columns, carrying the entablature on their heads. Around the cella block and north porch was a continuous frieze of separately-carved white marble figures attached by pins to a background of dark gray limestone. If the plan is awkward, or at least

Porch of the Maidens
Mary E. Dolbeare

unorthodox, the decorative elements, capitals, bases, antae, cornice moldings, door and window frames, and ceilings, are widely admired; the North Porch, in particular, has been described as the finest expression of the Ionic order, while visitors are inevitably drawn to the graceful Caryatid Porch.

The interior has been repeatedly gutted, but enough foundations remain to indicate that inside were four

(obscured) errant, ardent, actor; ch, chip; g, go; th, thin; ᵺ, then; y, you;
(variable) ḍ as d or j, ṣ as s or sh, ṭ as t or ch, ẓ as z or zh.

rooms on at least two levels. In addition to the cult of Athena Polias *(Protectress of the City)*, which we may locate in the E chamber, we learn that Poseidon and Hephaestus were worshiped there, and Pausanias also reports altars of Erechtheus, legendary founder of Athens, the name of whose chapel was eventually extended to the whole building, and his nephew Boutes, while beside the N porch was an altar of Zeus Hypatos. A fenced opening in the floor of the N porch permitted a view of markings in the native rock, said to have been made by Poseidon's trident in his contest with Athena for possession of Attica. To the west was the Pandroseum, in which stood the sacred olive tree.

The name of the architect of the Erechtheum is not recorded, but it has been observed that the complex design would give ample scope for the versatility displayed by Mnesicles, architect of the Propylaea. Construction was begun about 420 B.C., suspended in consequence of the Sicilian disaster of 413, resumed in 409, and completed probably in 405 B.C. It suffered from interior fires in the 4th century B.C. and at least twice in Roman times. In the Byzantine period it became a Christian church and during the Turkish domination it became the residence of the Pasha. Protracted researches by a commission of architectural historians of the American School of Classical Studies at Athens have resolved many of the problems of reconstruction and detail. (JJ)

Euphranor (ū-frā′nôr). Greek painter and sculptor in bronze and marble. He was born near Corinth, Greece, and was active in the middle of the 4th century B.C. His treatises on symmetry and color were much used by Pliny in the compilation of the 35th book of his *Natural History.* Lucian ranks his sculpture with that of Phidias, Alcamenes, and Myron, and his painting with that of Apelles, Parrhasius, and Aëtion. One of his most celebrated statutes was of Paris, the lover of Helen.

---

fat, fāte, fär, fåll, åsk, fāre; net, mē, hėr; pin, pīne; not, nōte, möve, nôr; up, lūte, půll; oi, oil; ou out; (lightened) ęlect, agǫny, ūnite;

Euphronius (ū-frō'ni-us). Celebrated Athenian potter and
vase-painter in the red-figure style, active at the end of
the 6th and the beginning of the 5th centuries B.C. Five
vessels signed by him as the painter and twelve signed

EUPHRONIUS
Heracles, red-figured volute crater, late 6th century B.C.
Museo Pubblico, Arezzo

by him as the potter are extant. A calyx crater (Louvre)
signed by him as the painter shows Heracles wrestling
Antaeus. The inside of a kylix (Munich), c510 B.C., is
decorated with a figure of a youthful horseman. Inscribed near the figure of the young rider is the name
Leagrus. Heracles slaying the triple-bodied Geryon is
shown on one side of the outside of the cup, and the
cattle of Geryon on the other. An inscription reads,
"Chachrylion made, Euphronius painted." Another
red-figured vessel by Euphronius (British Museum)
shows Eurystheus taking refuge in his brazen vessel as
Heracles attempts to deliver the Erymanthian boar to
him. The exploits of Heracles and Theseus were favorite subjects in the paintings of Euphronius, and on the

whole he favored the larger vessels—craters and amphorae—for his heroic subjects. It may be that Euphronius gave up painting for potting, for the vessels signed by him as potter are of somewhat later date than those signed by him as painter. The paintings on these vessels have been assigned to Onesimus, the Panaetius Painter, and the Pistoxenus Painter. Fiftynine cups have been attributed to Onesimus, some of which were thrown by Euphronius. Of the 41 vessels attributed to the Panaetius Painter, six were signed by Euphronius as potter. They include a kylix (Louvre) with a scene showing Theseus and Amphitrite under the sea, whither Theseus had gone to recover King Minos' ring. Eighteen works have been attributed to the Pistoxenus Painter, most of whose work comes somewhat after the time of Euphronius. One of the loveliest of these, in technique and feeling, is a white-

PISTOXENUS PAINTER
Aphrodite Riding on a Goose, white-ground cup, 500–475 B.C.
British Museum

ground cup interior (British Museum) showing Aphrodite riding a goose. Another of his masterpieces is a
cup (Athens) showing the death of Orpheus.

Eupompus (ū-pom′pus). Greek painter, born at Sicyon,
Greece, and active in the 4th century B.C. He was the
founder of the so-called Sicyonian school of painting.
The work of Eupompus and his successor Pamphilus
was to introduce the characteristics of Doric sculpture
into painting.

Euthymides (ū-thim′i-dēz). Celebrated Attic vase-painter,
active at the end of the 6th and the beginning of the
5th centuries B.C. Six vases with his signature as

EUTHYMIDES
Dancing Satyr, red-figured amphora, c510 B.C.
Munich

painter are extant. An amphora (Munich) c510 B.C., in
the red-figure style, shows three dancing satyrs on one
side, and is notable for the successful foreshortening
of the partly turned bodies of the satyrs. On this side

Euthymides, a contemporary, and perhaps a friendly rival, of Euphronius, inscribed a remark to the effect that Euphronius could never have painted anything like it. On the other side he painted Hector putting on his armor in the presence of Priam and Hecuba. On this side the inscription reads "Euthymides, son of Polios, painted." Another red-figured amphora (Munich) shows Theseus carrying off Corone. Other figures are identified by inscribed names as Helen, Pirithous, and Heres.

Exekias (ek-sē′ki-as). [Also: **Execias**.] Attic potter and painter in the black-figure style, active c550–525 B.C. He painted amphorae, craters, cups, and other vessels. Among his extant works are an amphora in the Vatican, showing Achilles and Ajax playing checkers, signed by him as both potter and painter; an amphora (Berlin), signed by him, showing the Dioscuri at home with Leda and Tyndareus; and a signed eye cup (Munich). The outside of the cup has two large eyes flanked by warriors near the handles; the inside shows Dionysus floating in a vine-swathed boat. The date of this cup, which is inscribed "Exekias made," is c540 B.C.

F

Farnese Bacchus (fär-nā′zā bak′us). Greek torso of the 4th century B.C., in the Museo Nazionale at Naples. It is of the school of Praxiteles.

Farnese Bull. A copy of a large group of Greek sculpture of the Trallian school (1st century B.C.), in the Museo Nazionale at Naples. It represents the chastisement of Dirce by her stepsons for her treatment of their mother, Antiope, by binding her to the horns of a bull.

fat, fāte, fär, fâll, ȧsk, fãre; net, mē, hėr; pin, pīne; not, nōte, möve, nôr; up, lūte, pull; oi, oil; ou out; (lightened) ẹlect, agōny, ūnite;

It is much restored, but is considered very remarkable for its composition and execution. It was discovered in the Baths of Caracalla in 1546 in a mutilated condition and was initially restored under the supervision of Michelangelo and later by the Milanese sculptor Bianchi.

Farnese Flora (flō′rạ). Ancient statue in the Museo Nazionale at Naples. The goddess holds her Ionian tunic with her right hand as she steps forward, the motif being a familiar one in archaic statues of Venus. The figure is considered remarkable for its grace, despite its height of 11½ feet.

Farnese Heracles (her′ạklēz) or *Hercules* (her′-kū-lēz). Greek statue in the Museo Nazionale at Naples executed by Glycon of Athens. The demigod is represented undraped, leaning on his club. The bearded head is somewhat small, and the muscular development prodigious. The statue, which is a copy of a Heracles by Lysippus, dates from the early empire (1st century B.C.).

Farnese Homer (hō′mėr). Ancient bust in the Museo Nazionale at Naples. Admirable in execution and remarkable for the profound intellectuality of its expression, it is perhaps the finest example of its familiar type, which is that universally associated with Homer.

Farnese Juno (jö′nō). Colossal antique bust of Juno (Hera), in the Museo Nazionale at Naples. The expression is one of calm repose, high and unbending. The hair is bound with a simple fillet. It has been demonstrated that this bust is probably a copy of a Hera made by Polyclitus (c423 B.C.) for the temple at Argos.

Farnese Minerva (mi-nėr′vạ). Greek statue of Pallas (Athena Parthenos), found at Velletri, Italy, and now in the Museo Nazionale at Naples. The type is that of the great statue of the Parthenon. The goddess wears the Attic helmet with a sphinx and two figures of Pegasus, and the aegis on her breast. The arms are restored; the right is extended to hold the Victory, and the left raised to sustain the spear.

(obscured) errạnt, ardẹnt, actọr; ch, chip; g, go; th, thin; ŦH, then; y, you;
(variable) ḍ as d or j, ṣ as s or sh, ṭ as t or ch, ẓ as z or zh.

Faun of Praxiteles (fôn; prak-sit′ęl-ēz). Ancient Greek statue by Praxiteles, the finest surviving copy of which is in the Capitoline Museum at Rome. The youth leans on a tree stump, nude except for a panther skin over the shoulder. The face betrays his animal kinship by little except the unusual hollow in the nose and the slightly pointed ears.

Ficoroni Cist (fē-kō-rō′nē). Cylindrical bronze box found near Palestrina, Italy, in 1745, and acquired by the Museo Kircheriano at Rome. It is important because its incised decoration, representing the victory of Polydeuces (Pollux) over Amycus, is one of the finest surviving examples of Greek line drawing. The box is over 1½ feet high, and rests on three feet; the handle of the cover is formed by a group consisting of Bacchus and two satyrs.

G

Gitiadas (ji-tī′ạ-dạs). Greek sculptor and architect who was active in the beginning of the 6th century B.C. Some say he constructed the bronze temple in which the bronze image of Athena was housed in Sparta, and for which reason she was called Athena Chalkioikos, "Of the Bronze House."

Glaucus (glô′kus). Greek sculptor in metals; fl. c6th century B.C. He lived at Chios but belonged to the Samian school of art. He is said to have been the inventor of the art of welding iron.

Glycon of Athens (glī′kon; ath′ęnz). Greek sculptor; fl. about the 1st century B.C. He made the Farnese Hercules, which was found in the Baths of Caracalla in 1540 with an inscription by Glycon. It was probably executed in the 1st century B.C. and is a copy of a Heracles by Lysippus.

Gnossus or *Gnosus* (nos′us). See *Cnossus*.

Graces, The Three. Antique undraped marble group preserved in the Opera del Duomo at Siena, Italy. It is the
foundation of many of the Renaissance and modern
representations of the subject.

——H——

Hageladas or ***Hagelaides*** (haj-e-lā′das). See ***Ageladas.***

Hecatompedon (hek-a-tom′pe-don). Popular name of an
early temple of Athena on the Acropolis at Athens. Its
foundations, buried beneath the Parthenon, cannot be
seen, but its dimensions and plan can be deduced from
its name (*hecatompedon* means "100-foot") and from
elements of the entablature and pediment sculptures
which have survived, and which indicate a date before
550 B.C., in the time of the Pisistratids. It was a modest
Doric temple of the limestone known as *poros*, restored
with tristyle-in-antis porches at front and rear. The
Hecatompedon was demolished between 490 and 480
B.C. to make way for a new and larger marble temple
of Athena, the "Older Parthenon," which in turn was
destroyed in scaffolding by the Persians in 480 B.C.

The name *Hecatompedon* is also used to designate the
cella of the third temple of Athena to rise on this spot,
the Parthenon, construction of which was begun in 447
B.C. Although the name implies that the Parthenon
cella was 100 feet in length, it was actually somewhat
less, 91½ Doric feet as measured by Dinsmoor; the
name doubtless arose from association with the Pisistratid Hecatompedon. (JJ)

Hegeso (hē-jē′sō), ***Monument of.*** Monument in Athens,
Greece, on the Street of Tombs, remarkable for the
beauty of its relief-stele of the 4th century B.C.

Helena (hel′e-na). Greek painter; daughter of the Egyptian Timon. She is said to have lived in the time of the

(obscured) errant, ardent, actor; ch, chip; g, go; th, thin; ŦH, then; y, you;
(variable) d as d or j, ş as s or sh, ţ as t. or ch, z as z or zh.

battle of Issus (333 B.C.), and to have painted a picture of that subject. This picture was hung by Vespasian in the Temple of Peace at Rome. The great Pompeian mosaic of the battle of Issus must have been made about this time, and is perhaps a copy of the picture.

MONUMENT OF HEGESO, 4TH CENTURY B.C.
National Museum, Athens
T.A.P. Service

Helladic (he-lad'ik). A term coined by prehistorians to
denote the material culture of the bronze age (c3000–
c1100 B.C.) of the mainland of Greece, and its three
chronological divisions: Early Helladic c3000–c1950
B.C., Middle Helladic c1950–c1650 B.C., Late Helladic
c1650–c1100 B.C., each in turn subdivided into two or
more phases. The term Mycenaean is synonymous
with Late Helladic in this context and is freely sub-
stituted for it. Parallel terms are Cycladic, denoting the
bronze-age culture of the islands of the Aegean (Cyclades), and Minoan, denoting the bronze-age culture
of Crete. (JJ)

Heraeum (hē-rē'um) or ***Heraion*** (-rī'on). National shrine
of the Argives, and one of the most sacred sanctuaries
of Hera, situated near Mycenae, in Argolis. It was to
this shrine that Cleobis and Biton pulled their mother
in a barrow so that, as a priestess, she could take part
in the rites. In the temple they went peacefully to sleep,
never to wake again. This was the answer the goddess
gave to their mother's prayer for a fitting reward for
her devoted sons. Some say it was at this temple, within
two miles of Mycenae, that Agamemnon heard the
vows of the Greek chiefs that they would take Troy or
die in the attempt. The site of the temple is on a slight
rise between the streams Eleutherios and Asterion.
The waters of the Eleutherios were employed by the
priestesses of the goddess in purification ceremonies.
The Argives claimed Hera was nursed by three daughters of the river-god Asterion, whose names were Euboea, Acraea, and Prosymna. On the banks of the river
grew a plant, also named asterion, which was offered
to Hera, and of which garlands were woven for the
image of the goddess. The ancient temple dated from
the 6th century B.C. This temple burned when, it is
said, a priestess tending the sacred fire fell asleep. A
new temple was built in its place (c423 B.C.), of which
the Argive Eupolemus was said to be the architect. The
new temple contained the celebrated chryselephantine

colossal statue of Hera by the sculptor Polyclitus. The ivory and gold seated image wore a crown on which were embossed figures of the Graces and the Horae. In one hand the goddess held a pomegranate, symbol of fertility; in the other hand she held a sceptor on which a cuckoo perched. The cuckoo signifies that Zeus first won Hera when he assumed the form of a cuckoo. Next to the goddess was an ivory and gold image of her daughter Hebe. Also in the temple was an ancient image made of wild pearwood, brought to the Heraeum

TWO CUCKOOS, 420–400 B.C.
Argive Heraeum

from Tiryns, which the Argives had conquered and destroyed. The silver altar in the precinct was decorated with a representation of the marriage of Hebe and Heracles. Before the temple were statues of former priestesses of the goddess, including one of the unfortunate priestess whose nap had brought destruction to the old temple. The shield Menelaus took from

Euphorbus at Troy was dedicated in the ancient temple, and in Roman times the Emperor Hadrian dedicated a peacock, bird sacred to Hera, made of precious stones in the new temple. Cleomenes, the Spartan king (c519–c487 B.C.), thought he had received assurance from an oracle that he would take Argos. He attacked the Argives near Tiryns and they fled for refuge into a sacred grove. As all efforts to force them out failed, Cleomenes set fire to the grove and burned them to death. Afterwards he asked the name of the grove. On learning that it was a grove sacred to Argus he feared that the oracle had been fulfilled, that he had taken the grove Argus and would not take the city Argos. He visited the Heraeum and made sacrifices to the goddess to learn whether he should proceed in his attempt to take Argos. When he made his offerings a flame flashed from the breast of the image of the goddess. This was a sign to Cleomenes that he should not attack Argos, for only if the fire flashed from the head of the image were the omens considered to be propitious. The Heraeum was excavated (1892–1895) by the American School at Athens, and more recently by the French School. A very valuable collection of archaic terra-cottas was recovered, as well as architectural and sculptural remains. The sculptures of the pediment depicted on one side the birth of Zeus and the war of the Giants, on the other the taking of Troy. Large fragments of these have been recovered.

Hermes Carrying the Infant Dionysus (hėr'-mēz; dī-ọ-nī'-sus). Subject of sculptured groups by several ancient artists, including one by Praxiteles which the Greek traveler Pausanias says he saw (c170 A.D.) in the Heraeum, or Temple of Hera, at Olympia. A superbly executed and well-preserved marble group found in the cella of the Heraeum by the German excavators was assumed at the time to be the group recorded by Pausanias and to be the original by Praxiteles. Since that day some experts have asserted that 1) the workman-

(obscured) errạnt, ardẹnt, actọr; ch, chip; g, go; th, thin; ᴛʜ, then; y, you;
(variable) ḍ as d or j, ṣ as s or sh, ṭ as t or ch, ẓ as z or zh.

ship and finish are not referrable to the time of Praxiteles, and 2) there is reason to think Praxiteles' original was of bronze; therefore, these scholars argue, the
group found was not the original, but a copy sub-
stituted in ancient times, conceivably after Pausanias'
visit. In the group, Hermes carries the babe on his left
forearm, which rests on a tree stump. His right hand,
now missing, held something which caught the child's
attention, probably a bunch of grapes. A greatly inferior adaptation of this group was found in the theater
of Minturnae in 1933. (JJ)

Hippodamus of Miletus (hi-pod′ạ-mus; mī-lē′-tus, mi-).
Greek architect and engineer, born c480 B.C., considered by the Greeks to have been the father of city-
planning. According to Aristotle, it was he who
introduced the principle of straight, wide streets and
the proper grouping of dwelling-places. The plans of
three cities were specifically attributed to him: Piraeus,
the port of Athens; Thurii, a colony established by
Athenians and others in 443 B.C. on or near the deserted site of Sybaris in the toe of Italy; and Rhodes.
At Piraeus and Rhodes, rectangular street plans have
in fact been detected, although it is not certain that
these go back to the 5th century B.C., and by 408 B.C.,
when Rhodes was laid out, Hippodamus would have
been at least 70 years old; Thurii has not been excavated. The checkerboard plan of Olynthus in Macedonia, dates from c425 B.C., during Hippodamus'
active period, and it has been suggested that this was
designed either by Hippodamus himself or by engi-
neers trained in his atelier. (JJ)

Hissarlik (hi-sär-lik′). See *Troy.*

Hydria (hī′dri-ạ). In ancient Greece, a large vase, used
especially for carrying water. It has a capacious body
with a narrow mouth and usually a broad rim, and
three handles: one at the back extending above the
rim, and a smaller one on each side.

—————I—————

Ictinus (ik-tī′nus). Greek architect; fl. in the middle of the 5th century B.C. With Callicrates, he was the chief designer of the Parthenon, begun 448 B.C., dedicated 438 B.C. He also designed the temple of Demeter and Persephone at Eleusis, and the temple of Apollo Epicurius at Bassae near Phigalia (the sculptured Ionic frieze of this temple is among the treasures of the British Museum). Ictinus and Phidias were identified· with Pericles in the execution of his great scheme of public works.

Ilion, Ilios, Ilium (il′i-ọn, -os, -um). Names for Troy, meaning the city founded by Ilus. See ***Troy***.

Ilium (il′i-um). See ***Troy***.

In antis (in an′tis). See ***Anta***.

Ionic Order (ī-on′ik). In architecture, one of the three Greek orders, so named from the Ionic race, by whom it was held to have been developed and perfected. The distinguishing characteristic of this order is the volute of its capital. In the true Ionic the volutes have the same form on the front and rear, and are connected on the flanks by an ornamented roll or scroll, except in the case of the corner capitals, which have three volutes on their two outer faces, that on the external angle projecting diagonally. The spiral fillets of the volute are continued along the face of the capital, beneath the abacus. The shaft, including the base and the capital to the bottom of the volute, is normally about nine diameters high, and is generally fluted in 24 flutes, separated by fillets. The bases used with this order are various. The Attic base often occurs, and is the most beautiful and appropriate. The architrave is normally formed in three bands, each projecting slightly beyond that below it, the whole crowned by a rich molding.

(obscured) errạnt, ardẹnt, actọr; ch, chip; g, go; th, thin; ꞪH, then; y, you; (variable) ḍ as d or j, ş as s or sh, ṭ as t or ch, ẓ as z or zh.

The frieze frequently bears figures in relief. The cornices fall under three classes: the simple but richly molded and strongly projecting Greek cornice, and the less refined dentil and modillion (Roman) cornices. Beautiful examples of the Ionic order are the Erechtheum and the Temple of Nike Apteros on the Acropolis at Athens. The details of the Erechtheum are

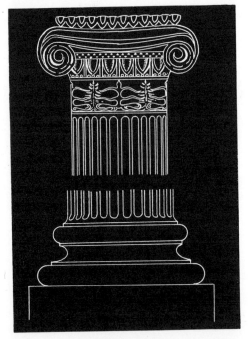

IONIC ORDER
A) volute; B) anthemion band; C) shaft; D) base

notable for the delicate elaboration of their ornament; but the interior capitals of the Propylaea are, in their simple purity of line, perhaps the noblest remains of the Greek Ionic. The order was probably evolved by the Ionian Greeks from forms found in Assyrian architecture.

—K—

Kalpis (kal'pis). A water-vase, usually of large size, resembling the hydria, and like it having three handles, but differing from the hydria in that the posterior handle does not extend above the rim.

KALPIS
Black-figured, Warriors Fighting, c510 B.C.
The Metropolitan Museum of Art

Knossos (nos'os). See *Cnossus.*
Korinthos (kô'rēn-thôs). See *Corinth* and *Corinthia.*
Kylix (kī'liks). [Also: *Cylix.*] In ancient Greece, a vase or cup of elegant form, used for drinking. The kylix was usually broad and shallow, with or without a slender foot, and provided with two handles not extending above the rim. Those with the slender foot closely resemble modern champagne glasses.

——L——

Laocoön (la-ok′ọ-on). Sculpture in the Vatican Museum, Rome, showing the Trojan priest of Apollo and his two young sons attacked by two great serpents, as narrated by Aeneas to Dido in Vergil's *Aeneid*, Book II, and frequently elsewhere. It is an important work of Hellenistic sculpture—Pliny the Elder regarded it as the greatest of all sculptures. According to Pliny, the sculptors were three, Agesander, Athenodorus, and Polydorus, all of Rhodes. It was discovered at Rome in 1506. (JJ)

Lecythus (les′i-thus) or ***Lekythos*** (lek′i-thos). A small oil- or perfume-vase of ancient Greece, of tall and graceful proportions and narrow neck. In Attica a particular class of lecythus was used, especially in funeral rites. The neck and the foot of these Attic lecythi are covered with black glaze, and the body has a clear white ground upon which are drawn with a brown outline figures and designs, often of remarkable delicacy and elegance. Unlike nearly all other examples of Greek vase-painting, these figures and designs are frequently filled out with bright and naturalistic colors.

Leochares (lẹ-ok′ạ-rēz). Athenian sculptor, who was active about the middle of the 4th century B.C. He was a pupil of Scopas and associated with him on the mausoleum of Halicarnassus. He is probably represented by the Ganymede and eagle of the Vatican, supposed to be a copy of his celebrated work.

Lion of Chaeronea (ker-ọ-nē′ạ). Colossal marble figure of a seated lion, erected by the Thebans over the common tomb of their troops who fell in the Battle of Chaeronea in 338 B.C., when Philip II of Macedon crushed the united armies of the Greek states and ended Greek resistance. In the 19th century a brigand

121

LEOCHARES
Battle of Greeks and Amazons, from the W frieze of the Mausoleum at Halicarnassus
British Museum

(obscured) errạnt, ardẹnt, actọr; ch, chip; g, go; th, thin; ŦH, then; y, you;
(variable) ḍ as d or j, ṣ as s or sh, ṭ as t or ch, ẓ as z or zh.

chief, hoping that the marble contained gold treasure, blew it up; in 1902 the fragmetns were reassembled, and the figure was eventually restored and replaced on its original pedestal. (JJ)

Lyceum (lī-sē'um). Gymnasium and exercise-ground of ancient Athens, lying on the right bank of the Ilissus, at the place now called Ilissia, a short distance E of the palace garden. It was a sanctuary of Apollo Lycius *(Wolfish)*. The story is that once when Athens was infested by wolves, Apollo ordered the people to sacrifice. They did so, and the smell of the sacrifice drove the wolves off. On the spot where the sacrifice was offered they dedicated the sanctuary and placed an image of Apollo Lycius in it. By the time of Pisistratus the Lyceum had become the chief gymnasium of Athens. It was noted for its fine groves of plane trees. Aristotle and his disciples formed the habit of discussing their philosophy while following the shady walks of this gymnasium, and hence received the name of Peripatetics. The Lyceum was burned in 200 B.C. by Philip V of Macedonia. The trees of the peaceful groves were cut down by Sulla (87–86 B.C.) to make siege engines when he was besieging Athens.

Lysicrates (lī-sik'rạ-tēz), *Choragic Monument of.* The best-preserved example of a type of structure once familiar at Athens, the choragic or choregic monument, built to commemorate a victory in a dramatic contest and to display the bronze tripod awarded the choragus who sponsored the winning production. The Monument of Lysicrates is circular in plan on a square stepped base. It has six Corinthian columns, the intercolumniations closed by curved slabs of marble so that the columns appear engaged, carrying an Ionic architrave, sculptured frieze, and cornice. Above this is a single conical roof block terminating in a rich ornamental anthemion which supported the tripod. The dedicatory inscription names the archon Evaenetus, in whose year the contest was held, corresponding to 330 B.C. (335 B.C., according to others). The monument stands beside what was then called the Street of Tripods, approaching the Theater of Dionysus from the east.

Of other choragic monuments near the theater, that of Thrasyllus, 320 B.C., survives in ruinous condition above the topmost seats of the theater, marked by a cave cut into the rock of the Acropolis. Another, erected by a choragus named Nicias, 320/319 B.C., was later dismantled, and many of its stones were used to build the lower gate (Beulē Gate), of Roman date, at the western entrance of the Acropolis, in whose structure they can still be seen. (JJ)

Lysippus (lī-sip'us). Greek sculptor, a native of Sicyon, who was active c372–316 B.C. According to Pliny he revised the canon of Polyclitus, making the head smaller and the legs longer, and adjusting details to a greater elongation. This new canon has been preserved in the *Apoxyomenus* of the Vatican, a young nude athlete scraping from his skin with a strigil the olive oil which took the place of soap in the bath, thought to be a copy of the bronze original placed by Agrippa before his baths in Rome. Lysippus also developed and fixed the extreme athletic type in Heracles, whom he repeatedly represented. A small table figure of Heracles in bronze was made for Alexander, who carried it about with him in his campaigns. It was afterward owned by Hannibal and Sulla. The *Torso Belvedere* is supposed to have been copied from this figure by Apollonius of Athens. Among the statues in bronze which Lysippus was said to have made was a colossal figure of Zeus at Tarentum. This was taken to the Capitol at Rome, removed from there to the Hippodrome in Constantinople, and melted down in the 11th century. There was also a colossal statue of the sun-god in a four-horse chariot, as well as a statue of Heracles, second in size only to the colossus of Rhodes. Through Chares of Lindus the characteristics of Lysippus were transmitted to the great Rhodian school which produced the *Laocoön.* Lysippus was the favorite sculptor of Alexander the Great, and author of most of his portraits in sculpture. An anecdote purporting to prove that, in an admittedly long and busy career, Lysippus made 1500 sculptures challenges credence.

——M——

Macron (mā′kron). Attic vase painter in the red-figure technique, active at the end of the 6th and the beginning of the 5th centuries B.C. He decorated all but three of 30 vessels signed by Hieron as potter. Two hundred and forty extant works have been attributed to him, among them a skyphos (Boston) showing Paris carrying off Helen, on one side, and Menelaus recovering her on the other. This vessel, signed by Macron as painter and Hieron as potter, is the only extant one on which the signature of Macron appears in its entirety.

Mausoleum (mô-sọ-lē′um). A magnificent tomb at Halicarnassus (Budrum) in SW Asia Minor, built for Mausolus, king of Caria, and his sister, wife, and queen, Artemisia, begun before Mausolus' death in 353 B.C. The names of the architects, Pythius and Satyrus, have been recorded, along with those of four famous sculptors, Bryaxis, Leochares, Scopas, and Timotheus. Vitruvius and Pliny have left summary descriptions from which it appears that the Mausoleum consisted of a colonnade, square in plan, surmounted by a pyramid, the latter crowned by a platform on which rested a marble four-horse chariot with statues of Mausolus and Artemisia by Pythius. Ancient critics acclaimed the whole as a great masterpiece and classed it among the seven wonders of the ancient world, so that thereafter any conspicuous monumental tomb might be called a mausoleum. The British Museum

SCOPAS

Battle of Greeks and Amazons, from the E frieze of the Mausoleum at Halicarnassus

British Museum

(obscured) errạnt, ardẹnt, actọr; ch, chip; g, go; th, thin; ŦH, then; y, you;
(variable) ḍ as d or j, ṣ as s or sh, ṭ as t or ch, ẓ as z or zh.

contains remains of three friezes and abundant other sculptures. (JJ)

Megaron (meg'ạ-ron). The great central hall of the Homeric house or palace. In large houses of this early time there was a *megaron* for the men and the entertainment of guests, and another, more secluded, for the women of the household. The plan and disposition of such megara, with the ceremonial family hearth in the middle, was clearly exposed in the excavations of Schliemann and Dörpfeld at Tiryns in the Peloponnesus.

Melanthus of Sicyon (mē-lan'thus; sish'i-on). [Also: *Melanthius*.] Greek painter (4th century B.C.), especially noted as a colorist, one of the great Sicyonian school founded by Eupompus. He was a pupil of Pamphilus. Like his teacher, he based his work on the scientific training which characterized the artistic activity of the Peloponnesian cities. He wrote a work much used by Pliny in the compilation of his thirty-fifth book.

Metope (met'ọ-pē). In architecture, a slab inserted between two triglyphs of the Doric frieze, sometimes, especially in late work, cut in the same block with one or more triglyphs. It was so called (*metope*, "opening," "window") because in the primitive Doric architecture in wood, of which the later triglyphs represent the ends of the ceiling-beams, the metopes were left open as windows, and were thus literally apertures between the beams. The metopes were often ornamented with paintings or with sculptures in high relief, but they were more usually left plain.

Metroum (mẹ-trō'um). A sanctuary of the Mother of the Gods (Rhea). The most celebrated was that of Athens, which stood at the foot of the hill known as Colonus Agoraeus, on the west side of the market-place or Agora. The story is that one of the begging priests of Rhea came to Athens and initiated the women into the rites of the Mother of the Gods. The Athenians did not understand the rites, and killed the priest by casting

fat, fāte, fär, fâll, àsk, fāre; net, mē, hẻr; pin, pīne; not, nōte, möve, nôr; up, lūte, pùll; oi, oil; ou out; (lightened) ẹlect, agǫny, ụnite;

him into a pit. At once plague broke out in Athens. The
oracle told the Athenians to propitiate the murdered
priest. To do so they built a shrine on the site of the
murder and dedicated it to the Mother of the Gods. In
the shrine they dedicated a statue of the begging
priest. It was a rule of this sacred precinct that no one
could enter it after eating garlic. Festivals called
Galaxia, at which a mixture of barley and milk was
eaten, were held here in honor of the Mother of the
Gods. In the Metroum was the large jar in which Diog-
enes was supposed to have lived. The Metroum was
the official depository of the state archives, including
such documents as a copy of the accusation against
Socrates, the plays of Aeschylus, Sophocles, and Euripides, and the will of the philosopher Epicurus. The
excavations in the Agora by the American School of
Classical Studies at Athens have revealed the foundations of an early temple, which was destroyed by the
Persians in 480 B.C. and not rebuilt, and an altar. On
this site was later built a group of buildings known as
the Metroum-Bouleuterium complex, a combination
of cult-place for the worship of the Mother of the
Gods, the state archives, and the *Bouleuterium,* or coun-
cil-house of the Five Hundred. Somewhere in this
complex stood a famous cult statue, attributed variously to Phidias or Agoracritus. (JJ)

Micon of Athens (mī'kon; ath'enz). Greek painter and
sculptor, active in the first half of the 5th century B.C.
He was a contemporary of Polygnotus, with whom he
worked in the Painted Portico *(Stoa Poikile)* at Athens.
In the Painted Portico he painted the *Battle of Theseus
and the Amazons.* In the picture of *The Battle of Marathon*
in the Painted Portico, on which he also worked, were
portraits of Callimachus, Miltiades, and possibly Aeschylus. On the walls of the Theseum he painted the
story of Theseus proving to Minos that he was a son
of Poseidon. When Theseus arrived in Crete with the
tribute of young maidens and young men from Athens,

(obscured) errant, ardent, actor; ch, chip; g, go; th, thin; FH, then; y, you;
(variable) d as d or j, s as s or sh, t as t or ch, z as z or zh.

Minos was attracted by one of the young girls and sought to seize her. Theseus rebuked him, claiming the right to do so as a son of Poseidon. Minos mocked him. He himself was a son of Zeus, he said, and called aloud to Zeus to give him a sign. There was an instant clap of thunder. Then Minos drew a ring from his finger and hurled it into the sea, telling Theseus that if he was indeed a son of Poseidon, he should leap into the sea and retrieve the ring. Theseus dived below the waters. Dolphins came to guide him and Nereids restored the ring. While under the sea he met Thetis, or as some say, Amphitrite, wife of Poseidon, who gave him a jeweled crown. With the ring and the crown he returned to Minos. He restored the ring to Minos and gave the crown to Ariadne as a bridal gift. Among other works by Micon was an incident from the voyage of Jason for the Golden Fleece that he painted in the temple of the Dioscuri at Athens, and a statue of the Athenian Callias, victor in Olympiad 77 (or 468 B.C.).

Minyan Ware (min'yạn). In the classification of ceramics which, in the absence of written records, is the principal basis of relative chronology in the Greek bronze age, two wheel-made wares widely associated with the Middle Bronze (Middle Helladic) Period are spoken of, perhaps inaccurately, as Minyan Ware. "Gray Minyan," the older of the two, dates from Middle Helladic 1, c1950–c1800 B.C. "Yellow Minyan" is associated with Middle Helladic 2, c1800-c1600 B.C. When heated sufficiently, Gray Minyan ware becomes yellow, suggesting that the change in fashion resulted simply from a technical improvement in the kiln which made possible a higher firing temperature. The cultural break which was once considered to close the Middle Helladic Period is no longer accepted. Archaeologists now consider that Middle Helladic 2 developed into the following period, Late Helladic 1 (Mycenaean 1), without a break, the earliest phases of the so-called Mycenaean pottery ware being essentially

fat, fāte, fär, fȧll, ȧsk, fãre; net, mē, hėr; pin, pīne; not, nōte, möve, nôr; up, lūte, pûll; oi, oil; ou out; (lightened) ḝlect, agǫny, ụnite;

Yellow Minyan ware to which decoration in color has been added. The name Minyan was applied to the gray ware by Heinrich Schliemann, who first identified it in his excavations at Boeotian Orchomenus, legendary seat of King Minyas. (JJ)

Mnesicles (nes'i-klēz). A brilliant Athenian architect of the Periclean period, known from literary sources to have been the designer of the magnificent *Propylaea,* or entrance-gates, of the Acropolis of Athens. The construction of the Propylaea was begun in 437 B.C. and left unfinished in 432 B.C., before the outbreak of the Peloponnesian War. From his skill and versatility in adjusting the design of the Propylaea to sloping ground, it has been suggested that Mnesicles was also the architect of the split-level *Erechtheum,* whose builder is otherwise unknown. (JJ)

Monopteron (mō-nop'tẹ-ron) or *Monopteros* (-ros). A type of Greek or Roman temple, usually circular and without an enclosed cella, composed of columns arranged in a ring and supporting a cupola or a conical roof. The temple of Rome and Augustus on the Acropolis of Athens, east of the Parthenon, was an example of a monopteron.

Museum (mū-zē'um). The name means "Sanctuary of the Muses," and so was applied not only to established shrines of the Muses but also loosely to schools dedicated to the pursuit of poetry, literature, rhetoric, philosophy, science, and music. In Athens, the Museum was a hill almost directly south of the Acropolis, the farthest E of the group of hills on the SW side of the city; named from an old shrine of the Muses located on it. On the summit stands a conspicuous monument, ornamented with niches, Corinthian columns, statues, and a relief-frieze, to Philopappus, grandson of the last king of Commagene, who became an Athenian citizen. The slopes of the hill, particularly on its southern extension, abound with curious rock-cuttings, for the most part vestiges of prehistoric Athens. These in-

(obscured) errạnt, ardẹnt, actọr; ch, chip; g, go; th, thin; ᴛʜ, then; y, you;
(variable) ḍ as d or j, ṣ as s or sh, ṭ as t or ch, ẕ as z or zh.

clude house foundations, stairs, meeting places with seats, and the so-called prison of Socrates and tomb of Cimon. Between this hill and the Pnyx passed the road to the Piraeus between the Long Walls. The rock is deeply cut by the ruts of chariot wheels and an artificial water channel.

Mycenae (mī-sē'nē). In ancient geography, a city in Argolis, Greece, about 14 miles SW of Corinth. It was a very ancient settlement, dating from perhaps the 20th century B.C., and was conspicuous in Greek legend and history. According to tradition, Argolis was inhabited by Pelasgians, who fell under the domination of Danaus when he arrived from Egypt with his 50 daughters. The kingdom of Danaus in Argolis was subsequently divided among his descendants. Acrisius became ruler of Argos. His brother Proetus ruled the neighboring region of Tiryns. When Perseus, grandson of Acrisius, unwittingly killed Acrisius, he did not wish to remain in Argos. He exchanged his inheritance with his cousin Megapenthes and became ruler of Tiryns. As Perseus proceeded toward Tiryns, he was overcome by thirst. He stooped to pluck a mushroom and drank the water from its cap. Pleased that he thus quenched his thirst, he founded a city on the spot and named it Mycenae for the mushroom *(mykos)*. Nearby the spot where this occurred is a spring, called by the ancients *Persea,* which still gives sparkling water to the inhabitants. Some say, however, that Perseus named his city from the cap of his sword, which happened to fall off at this spot, and which has a Greek name very similar to the word for mushroom. At all events, he fortified the city, which was on an eminence rising from the fertile plain, easily defendable and in a position to command routes to and from the sea. He secured the aid of the Cyclopes to build the wall of the city, which is sometimes called "the Cyclopean City," from the huge irregular stones that form its wall. Sthenelus, son and successor of Perseus, received

Atreus and Thyestes, sons of Pelops, into his realm when they fled from their father. On the death of Eurystheus, son of Sthenelus, Atreus became king, ended the Perseid dynasty and established that of the Pelopidae, which became the equal of any kingdom in the Peloponnesus. Signs of fire found in the excavations at Mycenae are attributed to the struggles that took place when Atreus assumed mastery. Atreus was followed by his brother Thyestes, who in turn was succeeded by Agamemnon, son of Atreus and brother of Menelaus. The rulers between Perseus and Agamemnon cover the period of time between about the middle of the 14th century, when the city was founded by Perseus, and the fall of Troy, the traditional date of which is 1183 B.C. In the time of Agamemnon, Mycenae was at its apogee. Tiryns, Argos, and Midea were subject to him, as was most of the Peloponnesus and the neighboring islands. As master of a strong maritime empire he exercised influence over most of the Greek mainland and the islands, and drew supporters from the entire area when he led the expedition to Troy to recover Helen. The murder of Agamemnon on his return from his successes at Troy by his wife Clytemnestra and her lover Aegisthus, provides the material for some of the most dramatic pages of Greek tragedy. After an interval in which Mycenae was ruled by Clytemnestra and Aegisthus, Agamemnon was succeeded by his son Orestes and his grandson Tisamenus. During the reign of Tisamenus the Dorians invaded the Peloponnesus, took Mycenae, and destroyed its citadel. Thereafter, the influence and power of Mycenae was in eclipse.

As in many cases, history and legend are closely intertwined at Mycenae. Archaeologists consider that the earliest city to occupy the site dated from about the 20th century B.C. In succeeding centuries close relations were established between Mycenae and Crete, and remains of a distinctly Cretan character, dating

---

(obscured) errạnt, ardẹnt, actọr; ch, chip; g, go; th, thin; ᵺн, then; y, you; (variable) ḍ as d or j, ṣ as s or sh, ṭ as t or ch, ẓ as z or zh.

from 1600–1400 B.C., have been found in tombs on the site along with other evidences of Cretan domination in this period. Following the establishment of the city of Perseus, c1350 B.C., a distinctively Mycenaean culture developed throughout the area and spread to Asia Minor in the east and to Sicily in the west. In the period of its greatness the kings of Mycenae were the peers of the kings of Egypt and Babylon. From the end of the 12th century B.C. the importance of Mycenae declined so completely that nothing more is heard of it until the Persian Wars, when 80 Mycenaeans went to the aid of Leonidas at Thermopylae and later 200 shared in the victory at Plataea (479 B.C.). The Argives, roused to jealousy by the pride which the Mycenaeans took at having their names inscribed on the tripods at Delphi after the Battle of Plataea, attacked Mycenae and destroyed it c470 B.C. The city never recovered from this attack. Only a village remained on the site. The traveler and writer Pausanias visited there in the 2nd century A.D., and saw parts of the old walls and the Lion Gate (which was never completely obscured). He also claimed to have seen the graves of Atreus and Agamemnon in the citadel, as well as the graves of Clytemnestra and Aegisthus outside the walls (for they, as murderers, could not be buried in the citadel). Modern scholars doubt that Pausanias actually saw the graves, for they must have been covered over; rather, it is thought that they were described to him by local inhabitants who knew of them by tradition. From the time of Pausanias until the 19th century Mycenae was a forgotten village. In that century the site was rediscovered by travelers, and various objects that were uncovered were carried off. It was not until the end of the century that the city as a famous and immensely valuable historical and archaeological site again came to the attention of the world. The original excavations were made by Heinrich Schliemann in 1876–77. Following the account of Pausanias, Schliemann discov-

ered the Grave Circle of Mycenae with its royal shaft
graves. Five graves were rapidly cleared and yielded a
rich treasure. Later work was done on the site by the
Archaeological Society of Athens. The Mycenae of the
Iliad, "that well-built city and fortress," the "golden,"
"wide-wayed" city especially loved by Hera, as well as
the city of much earlier times, has been steadily emerg-
ing through archaeological expeditions ever since, notably those undertaken by the British Archaeological
Society under Prof. A. J. B. Wace, which were inter-
rupted in 1939 by the outbreak of World War II, and
those of the Greek Archaeological Society in the
1950's. In the latest excavations (1952 and following
years), a new grave circle has been disclosed, which
includes the graves of the ruling families of the 17th
and 16th centuries B.C. The shaft graves found by
Schliemann and those in the new grave circle uncovered in 1952 were cut into the rock, sealed off, and
covered over. They contained many skeletons and objects of value that decorated the bodies of the dead
when they were interred. This is of interest as it shows
that at the time of these burials the Mycenaeans did not
burn their dead, as they did according to the Homeric
poems of a later age. Rather, they buried them with all
the accoutrements of the living—ornaments, utensils,
and weapons. However, once the flesh had disappeared from their bones, no more concern was expressed for their souls or for their journey to the other
world, and it appears that the skeletons were somewhat unceremoniously moved to one side to make
room for new arrivals in the tombs. Excavations at the
site of Mycenae have supplied some of the oldest
materials for the study of Greek architecture and art.
The site consisted of an acropolis, occupying the apex
of a hill, and the lower town, the confused ruins of
which are spread over its slopes. The acropolis is triangular, and is surrounded by a massive wall of huge
stones (Cyclopean stones), partly shaped. It is entered

(obscured) errạnt, ardẹnt, actọr; ch, chip; g, go; th, thin; ᴛʜ, then; y, you;
(variable) ḍ as d or j, ṣ as s or sh, ṭ as t or ch, ẓ as z or zh.

by the Gate of the Lions, which dates from the 14th
century B.C. This gate is at the end of a walled passage
so placed that the right, or unshielded, side of an
enemy would be exposed to the defenders within the
citadel. The opening of the gate is about ten feet wide

Lion Gate, 14th century B.C.
Greek National Tourist Office

and high, tapering toward the top, with monolithic jambs and a huge lintel. Above the lintel a large triangular opening is formed by corbeling, and the great slab, two feet thick, which fills this, bears the remarkable relief of two facing rampant lions separated by a column. Close inside of this gate, in a double circle of upright stones 80 feet in diameter, were found shaft graves containing golden ornaments and masks, inlaid

So-called Mask of Agamemnon, early 15th century B.C.
Greek Embassy Press and Information Service

swordblades, and other objects whose discovery astonished the scientific world. According to legend, these were the tombs of Atreus, Electra, Agamemnon, Cassandra, and others of the period. Modern scholars place the date of the tombs earlier than the time of

(obscured) errănt, ardĕnt, actor; ch, chip; g, go; th, thin; ŦH, then; y, you;
(variable) ḏ as d or j, ş as s or sh, ṭ as t or ch, ẓ as z or zh.

Agamemnon, between the 19th and 16th centuries B.C. Excavations have disclosed on the acropolis a prehistoric palace resembling that at Tiryns, and remains of palaces and temples of later periods that were superimposed on it. Remains still exist of the ramp on which, perhaps, Clytemnestra placed the royal purple for the feet of Agamemnon on his triumphant return from Troy. The bath in which she almost immediately thereafter slew him disappeared when part of the acropolis was destroyed in a landslide. This is the acropolis that the tutor points out to Orestes, in Sophocles' *Electra,* as "a treasure-house of gold . . . the ancestral home of the family of Pelops, a house of death if ever there was one." The most important monuments of the lower town are the great "beehive" tombs, commonly called treasuries. Of these, one sometimes called "the treasury of Atreus" and sometimes "the tomb of Agamemnon," is a typical example. The interior is a circle about 50 feet in diameter and slightly less in height, covered with a pseudodome formed by corbeling in the horizontal courses of the wall. Indications are that the inner surface of the tomb was decorated with medallions in metal and painted designs. The discoveries at Mycenae threw a flood of light upon the earliest Greek art, particularly in pottery. They were the first important finds of their class, which has since been recognized in a large proportion of Greek settlements of sufficient age, and is everywhere distinguished as Mycenaean. Mycenaean ornament includes geometric decoration, foliage, marine and animal forms, and the human figure. Mycenaean art was practiced and developed through several centuries, and existed contemporaneously with the succeeding dipylon style of decoration, which began c1000 B.C. Among the objects found in the second grave circle, excavated 1952 and following years, are: bronze daggers, spears, swords, and the remains of a leather scabbard; pottery, including painted vases, am-

---

fat, fāte, fär, fȧll, ȧsk, fãre; net, mē, hèr; pin, pīne; not, nōte, mŏve, nôr; up, lūte, pu̇ll; oi, oil; ou out; (lightened) ḝlect, agǫny, ūnite;

phorae, and jars; engraved gems; gold ornaments, including bands, buttons, and ear clips; beads of semi-precious stones; rock crystal bowls and pins with rock crystal heads; and gold cups. In 1970 it was reported that remains of several Bronze Age frescoes had been discovered in the ruins of a house believed to have been destroyed about 1200 B.C. A two-foot section of one fresco, now undergoing restoration, depicts a half-figure of a goddess or priestess; there were also fragments found of stylized motifs previously found only in palaces and royal houses. The chief objects found at Mycenae are in the National Museum at Athens.

Myron (mī′rŏn). Greek sculptor; fl. c450 B.C. He was a native of Eleutherae on the frontier between Attica and Boeotia, and a pupil of Ageladas of Argos. Polyclitus and Phidias were reputedly his fellow pupils. Myron worked, exclusively or primarily, in bronze, a medium which released the artist from the static poses of sculpture in marble and made possible the athlete statues for which he became famous. He considered the subject more from the standpoint of action than of proportion, and represents the attitudes of the active rather than the beauty of the passive athlete. In this he was considered supreme. His most representative work was probably the *Discobulus* or discus-thrower, described by Quintilian and Lucian, of which inadequate copies can be seen in the British Museum, the Vatican, and the National Museum (Museo delle Terme) in Rome. His group of Athena and Marsyas is represented by the Athena in Frankfurt and the Marsyas of the Lateran, as well as on coins and on a marble vase in Athens. Myron's bronze cow on the Pnyx at Athens was a popular Greek and Roman favorite. (JJ)

Mys (mis). Greek artist who was active in the latter part of the 5th century B.C. He was famous for chasing designs on or working reliefs on metal. From a design of Parrhasius he engraved the battle between the

Lapiths and Centaurs on the inside of the shield of the great bronze statue of Athena Promachus on the Acropolis. From another design of Parrhasius he made the Sack of Troy in relief on a cup.

Myson (mī′son). Attic potter and painter, active early 5th century B.C. Forty-seven extant vessels are attributed to him. One of the finest of these is an amphora (Louvre) showing Croesus on his pyre. It is in the red-figure technique.

——N——

Naos (nā′os). "Dwelling-place"; the Greek word for temple (Latin *aedes*), the stately residence reserved for a god on his visits to the community. The term is also applied to the principal chamber of a temple, in which stood the image of the god and where the valuable properties of the cult were stored (Latin *cella*). Except for a few circular temples *(tholoi)*, Greek temples were generally rectangular, with the long axis running east to west (but north to south at Bassae) and the entrance at the east. Rarely we hear of altars within the cella. The main altar, at which important sacrifices were performed, regularly stood in the open air facing the entrance; a temple sanctuary *(temenos)* might, however, contain several subsidiary altars and occasionally small buildings of temple form called treasuries. The simplest form of Greek temple is a single room with an open (prostyle) or partly enclosed (in-antis) columned porch. Embellishments may take the form of porches at both front and rear (amphiprostyle), or colonnades completely surrounding the cella (peristyle). (JJ)

Nearchus (nē-är′kus). Attic painter and potter in the black-figure style, active c570 B.C. Over 40 cups with his signature are extant. He was one of the foremost makers and painters of the Little Master cups, so-called because of the exquisite miniature paintings that decorated them. A fragment of a cantharus (Athens) signed by him, shows Achilles and parts of three horses and represents the moment when Achilles was preparing to rejoin the battle against the Trojans to avenge Patroclus.

Nereid Friezes (ner′ē-id). Four friezes from the Nereid monument at Xanthus in Lycia, now in the British Museum. The widest frieze represents a battle between Greeks and Asiatics; the others represent episodes of war, the chase, banquet, and sacrifice.

Nesiotes (nes-i-ō′tēz, nē-shē-). See *Critius and Nesiotes.*

Nicias of Athens (nish′i-as; ath′enz). Greek painter of the 4th century B.C., a younger contemporary of Praxiteles. When Praxiteles was asked which of his works in marble he valued most, he is said to have answered, "Those on which Nicias has set his mark." Pliny explains this expression by the comment, "So much importance did Praxiteles attach to the *circumlitio* (tinting of color) applied by Nicias." This passage was for a long time the principal foundation for the theory that the Greeks painted their statues, which is now confirmed by the works themselves. Nicias was noted for his skill in giving a third dimension to his pictures by the proper use of light and shade, and was celebrated for his painting of female figures and other subjects which gave scope for dramatic treatment. Among the latter was a *Rescue of Andromeda* and one of *Odysseus Questioning the Dead in the Underworld.* Ptolemy of Egypt offered a large sum for this latter picture, but Nicias preferred to make a present of it to Athens.

Nicomachus (nī-kom′a-kus). Greek painter, active about the middle of the 4th century B.C. He was noted for the speed and excellence with which he painted. One of his paintings famous in antiquity was *The Rape of Persephone.*

(obscured) errant, ardent, actor; ch, chip; g, go; th, thin; ŦH, then; y, you;
(variable) d as d or j, s as s or sh, t as t or ch, z as z or zh.

Nicosthenes (ni-kos′thi-nēz). Attic potter of the 6th century B.C. His work is known from about 100 extant vessels bearing his signature. The decorator of his vessels worked in the black-figure style and is called the Nicosthenes Painter.

Nike Apteros (nī′kē, nē′kā; ap′tẹ-ros) or *Wingless Victory, Temple of.* See *Athena Nike, Temple of.*

Niobids (nī′ọ-bidz). The term means "Children of Niobe." The *Slaughter of the Niobids,* when Apollo and Artemis avenged Niobe's affront to their mother Leto by slaying Niobe's seven sons and seven daughters with their arrows, attracted at least two able sculptors. Copies of individual figures by them, separated by considerations of style into a 5th-century B.C. group and a 4th-century B.C. group, survive in European museums. Assigned to the 5th-century group is the superb Niobid in the National Museum (Museo delle Terme) in Rome, and a boy and a girl in Copenhagen. A collection of 18 statues in the Uffizi in Florence, the Chiaramonti Niobid in the Vatican, and others are assigned to the 4th-century group. The theme, offering a variety of postures, standing, running, crouching, kneeling, and prostrate, with perhaps 18 figures (Apollo, Artemis, Niobe, 14 children, and the *paedagogus* or tutor), would have lent itself admirably to the triangular composition of a temple pediment, and it is likely that one or both groups were originally so designed and erected, to be eventually shipped to Rome. It has been suggested that the 5th-century group represents the missing S pediment of the temple of Apollo at Bassae. The identification of the sculptors is in dispute. (JJ)

Odeum (ō̆-dē′um). "Singing-place." The odeum was a form of roofed theater, generally smaller than the great open-air theaters of Greece and Rome. It was developed primarily for musical performances, because the volume of sound produced by early stringed and reed instruments was insufficiently audible in open-air theaters. The earliest recorded example is the Odeum of Pericles at Athens, built in the 5th century B.C., burned in the 1st century B.C., and reconstructed by Ariobarzanes II, king of Cappadocia. Agrippa built an odeum in the Athenian Agora, and in the 2nd century A.D. Herodes Atticus built odea at Athens and Corinth. In the absence of special buildings for the purpose, an odeum could conveniently serve as a meeting-place for a *bouleuterium* (town council) or *ecclesiasterium* (public assembly), and with this versatility odea were widely built throughout the Roman provinces. (JJ)

Odeum of Herodes Atticus (hē̆-rō′dēz at′i-kus). A roofed theater at Athens, at the SW foot of the Acropolis. It was built in the middle of the 2nd century A.D. at the expense of the wealthy statesman, litterateur, and art patron Herodes Atticus, in memory of his wife Regilla, for whom it is sometimes called the Odeum of Regilla. It is of Roman plan, semicircular, about 260 feet in diameter, with about 33 rows of seats and well-preserved stage and scene. As elsewhere, the revetment of the seats and scene-building, pavement, etc., were removed before the liberation of Greece from the Turks, but are currently being restored, and the odeum is again used for dramatic presentations, concerts, etc. Herodes Atticus also built an odeum at Corinth. (JJ)

Oenochoë (ē-nok'ọ̄-ē). In Greek antiquity, a small vase of graceful shape, with a three-lobed rim, the central lobe forming a mouth adapted for pouring, and a single handle reaching above the rim: used for dipping wine from the crater and filling drinking cups.

Oltos (ol'tos) ***Oltus*** (-tus). Attic vase-painter, active c530–510 B.C. Two kylixes (cups) signed by him as the painter are extant, and over 100 other cups have been attributed to him. Among his works is a large kylix (Tarquinia) on which the gods on Olympus are shown.

OLTOS
Red-figured eye-cup, c530–520 B.C.
Munich

An eye cup (Munich) decorated on the inside in black-figure style shows Dionysus with a drinking cup; on the outside the decoration is in red-figure and consists of two large eyes separated by a flute case on one side and two large eyes separated by a nose on the other. Another cup (Munich) in red-figure has Priam with a train of gift bearers before Achilles to ransom the body of Hector. Oltos also worked, to a less degree but with great success, on the larger vessels, as the amphora and stamnos.

Olympia (ọ̄-lim'pi-ạ). In ancient geography, the site of a celebrated sanctuary of Zeus and of the Olympic Games, the most important of the great public games of classical antiquity. Situated in Elis in the valley of the Alpheus River at its confluence with the Cladeus River, its location and importance caused it to be spared the incessant warfare that harassed most of the rest of Greece. The area was originally a part of Pisatis, whose

capital was Pisa, but came, after many engagements
between Eleans, Pisans, Spartans, and Argives, under
the control of Elis early in the 6th century B.C.
Through centuries of warfare and change in Greece,
Olympia remained a relatively peaceful spot, remote
from political upheavals and protected by its geo-
graphical location. It was primarily a religious center,
where the athletic contests in honor of the gods gradually took on more importance than the religious ceremonies that brought them into being. The site is a
peaceful valley, cooled by numerous pine trees, once
washed by two rivers, and protected at the north by the
low wooded Hill of Cronus. The origins of the sanctuary and of the games are anterior to history; according
to tradition the games were reorganized, in obedience
to the Delphic oracle, in the 9th century B.C. The list
of Olympic victors goes back to 776 B.C., which is the
first of the four years of the first Olympiad, but the
Olympiad system of chronology did not come into accepted use until much later. South of the Hill of
Cronus at Olympia was the Altis, a sacred enclosure
that was the religious center. It was surrounded by a
low wall, the location of which was changed from time
to time through the centuries to enlarge the enclosure.
Inside the Altis was the 6th century B.C. Doric temple
of Zeus, built from the spoils that were taken from the
Pisans by the Eleans. Libo, the architect who designed
the temple shortly after the Elean victory, did not live
to see its completion, which was not accomplished until the middle of the 5th century B.C. The greatest
treasure of the temple, which was richly decorated
within and without, was the statue of *Olympian Zeus* by
Phidias. In front of the temple, facing the east, were
many statues given as votive offerings at various times.
Among them was the *Nike* of Paeonius, given by the
Messenians to celebrate a victory over the Spartans.
Inside the north wall of the Altis was the ancient temple of Hera, in the cella of which stood the famous

(obscured) errant, ardent, actor; ch, chip; g, go; th, thin; ŦH, then; y, you;
(variable) ḍ as d or j, ş as s or sh, ṭ as t or ch, ẓ as z or zh.

NIKE OF PAEONIUS, 5TH CENTURY B.C.
Olympia Museum
Greek Embassy Press and Information Service

fat, fāte, fär, fȧll, ȧsk, fãre; net, mē, hėr; pin, pīne; not, nōte, mȯve, nôr; up, lūte, pull; oi, oil; ou out; (lightened) ḝlect, agȯny, ūnite;

Hermes and the Infant Dionysus, by Praxiteles. Between the temples of Zeus and Hera, on a slight rise, was a sanctuary of Pelops, enclosed by a pentagonal stone wall. Black rams were here sacrificed to Pelops, who was honored at Olympia only slightly less than Zeus, and in memory of whom, some say, the first games were instituted. East of the temple of Hera stood the *Metroum,* a temple dedicated to the Mother of the Gods, and south of the Metroum, roughly in the middle of the Altis, was a very ancient altar of Zeus made of ashes of victims mixed with the waters of the Alpheus River. In addition, there was a profusion of statues of gods, heroes, and victors scattered within the Altis, as well as numerous other buildings that were erected in later times. Outside the Altis, to the west, was the *Bouleterium,* dating from the 6th and 5th centuries B.C. Here sat the Upper Council, or Boule, that managed affairs at Olympia. Also to the west were a gymnasium and palestra where the athletes trained for the contests. At the northwest corner of the Altis stood the *Prytaneum,* the chief administrative building at Olympia, where the priests and other officials took their meals and where visitors of importance and victors were entertained. In half the building was the sacred hearth of Hestia, on which a fire was kept burning at all times. To the east of the Altis was the stadium, capable of seating 20,000 spectators, where the foot races were held. German archaeologists have uncovered the marble starting line, marked off in equal spaces for the contestants, and the finish line, 192.27 meters away. South of the stadium was the hippodrome, where the chariot races were run. In addition, the site at Olympia was occupied by a number of *thermae,* chiefly of Roman date, the treasuries of various Greek cities and states, numberless statues and works of art, and steles with commemorative inscriptions. The Olympic Games were formally abolished (394 A.D.) by the emperor Theodosius as a relic of pagan-

(obscured) errạnt, ardẹnt, actọr; ch, chip; g, go; th, thin; ᵺн, then; y, you; (variable) ḍ as d or j, ş as s or sh, ṭ as t or ch, ẓ as z or zh.

ism. The monuments were much shattered by earthquakes in the 6th century, and as time went on were
progressively buried by landslides from Cronus and

Temple of Hera, c7th century B.C.
Greek National Tourist Office

inundations of the Cladeus (now dry), and the Alpheus, in one of which the hippodrome was entirely
washed away. Sand and earth were deposited to a
depth of from ten to 20 feet over the ruins. Nor was
man free from responsibility in the destruction of the
monuments. The heads of many statues were lopped
off to destroy the pagan idols, and much material from
the temples and other buildings was carried away for
use in humbler structures. The French *Expédition de
Morée* made (1829) some superficial excavations, and
recovered some sculptures (now in the Louvre) from
the temple of Zeus. In six seasons of work after 1874,
the German government laid bare down to the ancient
level the greater part of what survives of the sanctuary.
The sculptural finds include the *Hermes* of Praxiteles
and the *Nike* of Paeonius, which are now in the Museum at Olympia, along with large fragments from the

fat, fāte, fär, fåll, àsk, fāre; net, mē, hèr; pin, pīne; not, nōte, möve,
nôr; up, lūte, pùll; oi, oil; ou out; (lightened) ĕlect, agǫny, ūnite;

pediments of the temple of Zeus as well as fragments of metopes from the same temple. In the departments of architecture and epigraphy the German excavations, resumed after World War II, rank as the most important that have been made. The antiquities discovered are preserved on the site. Olympia as a religious and athletic center did not seek to exercise influence on political affairs, and it was perhaps for this reason that it was respected as a peaceful island in the midst of the

APOLLO
From the W pediment of the Temple of Zeus, Olympia
T.A.P. Service

constantly warring Greek city-states, that armed soldiers were not permitted to pass through its territory, and that guarantees of safe conduct through hostile areas could be given to contestants and spectators going to the games. For centuries, the festival at Olympia gave one point of unity to the Greeks perpetually at odds with each other. In its Golden Age, Olympia developed a high standard of personal excellence in the games, and served as a widely-attended showplace for the presentation of Greek ideas and for the exhibition of some of the finest achievements in Greek art, poetry, literature, and philosophy.

Olympian Zeus. Great statue of Zeus in the sanctuary at Olympia. It was one of the Seven Wonders of the Ancient World, and in ancient times it was considered a misfortune to have died without beholding it. The statue, of ivory and gold, with painted draperies, was made by Phidias, whose workshop near the sanctuary at Olympia existed into the Christian era and later became a Byzantine church. Phidias was assisted in executing the statue, which was considered, with the statue of Athena in the Parthenon, his masterwork. According to tradition, when Phidias was commissioned to make the statue he was asked what model he would use, and was said to have replied that he would use Homer's description:

> "Thus spoke the son of Cronus, and with darkling eyebrows he nodded.
> Then the ambrosial locks of the King flowed waving about him,
> Down from his head immortal; . . ."

When the statue was finished, Phidias prayed for a sign from Zeus that the god found it acceptable. Immediately a bolt of lightning struck the floor of the temple in front of the image, signifying the pleasure of Zeus in the work. Many eminent travelers of the ancient world testified to the extraordinary beauty and majesty of the statue, but only Pausanias attempted to describe it in detail. He tells of the god on his throne, his head wreathed with the wild olive. In his right hand was an image of Victory; in his left hand was an ornamented scepter on which perched an eagle. On his feet were golden sandals, and his robe was decorated with figures of animals and flowers. The throne was of gold, jewels, ebony, and ivory, and was decorated with many figures from mythology. According to some accounts, the Emperor Caligula wished to transport the image to Rome, and replace the head of Zeus with an image of his own, but the ship he sent for the purpose was struck by lightning and lost. Whenever, later, any of his men attempted to lay hands on the statue, they were driven back by a loud peal of laughter from the image. The image has been completely lost. Some say it was lost in a fire about 408 A.D. or that it was destroyed in Constantinople, whither it had been taken, about 475 A.D. Only representations of it on coins remain. The descendants of Phidias held the office of Burnishers of the Image for generations; they anointed the ivory with oil to keep it from cracking.

Onatas (ō-nā'tas). Aeginetan sculptor and painter, a contemporary of Ageladas, the teacher of Phidias. He was active c500–460 B.C. He was especially famous for his statues of athletes. Pausanias has described many of his works, as the *Apollo* of Pergamum, the *Ten Greek Heroes* casting lots to see which would take up the challenge of Hector to single combat, and a group representing Hiero of Syracuse in the chariot in which he won the victory at the Olympic Games.

Onesimus (ō-nē'si-mus). See *Euphronius,* painter and potter.

Opisthodomus (op-is-thod'ō-mus). In Greek architecture, an open vestibule within the portico at the end behind the cella in most ancient temples, corresponding to the pronaos at the principal end, into which opens the main entrance. It was sometimes used as a place for preserving the temple treasure.

Orchomenus (ôr-kom'e̯-nus). In ancient geography, a city in Boeotia, Greece, situated on the Cephissus River, about 55 miles NW of Athens. It became a member of the Boeotian Confederacy at the beginning of the 7th century B.C. In the Persian War it was on the side of the Persians. Up to the time of the Peloponnesian Wars,

(obscured) errạnt, ardẹnt, actọr; ch, chip; g, go; th, thin; ᵵн, then; y, you; (variable) ḍ as d or j, ş as s or sh, ṭ as t or ch, ẓ as z or zh.

Orchomenus was the equal of Thebes, but following that long struggle Thebes became a democracy, and the aristocracy that ruled Orchomenus took the side of Sparta and became an enemy of Thebes, fighting against that city at Coronea and Haliartus. When the Thebans defeated Sparta at Leuctra (371 B.C.) they would have destroyed Orchomenus, but Epaminondas persuaded them to spare it. However, in 364 B.C. they destroyed it without mercy. It was rebuilt in 353 B.C. by the Phocians, but was destroyed again by the Thebans in 349 B.C. Philip of Macedon rebuilt it anew, but the city never recovered its former power and wealth. In 87 B.C., Sulla defeated Archelaus, the general of Mithridates VI, king of Pontus, before the walls of Orchomenus. The site contains important remains of antiquity, going back to the Neolithic Age. Modern excavations have uncovered one city built atop another, as at Troy, the oldest of which dates from before 3500 B.C. Fragments of vases and frescoes, on which are depicted buildings and scenes of bull-leaping, and designs similar in style to those of Cnossus and Tiryns, have been recovered at the site. The so-called treasury of Minyas is a very ancient tomb of the Mycenaean beehive type. The plan is circular, 45 feet in diameter, covered by a pseudo-dome formed by corbeling in the stones of the wall. The approach to the tomb is a walled dromos, or entrance passage. The actual burial chamber was a separate, rectangular room cut into the living rock and reached by a tunnel leading from the circular structure. Plaques of palmettes, rosettes, and other decorative elements, cut from green schist, ornament the walls and ceiling of this chamber, and are in mint condition.

Orpheus, Eurydice, and Hermes (ôr′fūs; ôr′fẹ̄-us; ụ-rid′i-sē; hėr′mēz). Replica of an Attic high relief of the school of Phidias, in the Museo Nazionale, Naples. The group is shown just at the moment when Orpheus, having looked back, must lose his wife forever.

P

Paeonius (pē-ō′ni-us). Greek sculptor of Mende in Thrace, active in the latter part of the 5th century B.C. Some say he was one of the sculptors who worked on the decorations of the temple of Zeus at Olympia, and among the figures by him there was a group representing the chariot race between Pelops and Oenomaus. Paeonius made the statue of Victory which the Messenians dedicated at Olympia in honor of the defeat of their ancient enemies the Spartans at Sphacteria and Cythera (425 B.C.), and in celebration of their part in the defeat. The statue, a contemporary marble copy of a bronze original, was discovered in 1875 with its inscription, and gives a perfect idea of this master's style.

Paestum (pes′tum). City in Lucania, in southern Italy,

Temple of Poseidon and Basilica
Italian State Tourist Office

situated near the sea. Founded as Posidonia, a colony of Sybaris, c600 B.C., it quickly achieved prosperity, as its great Doric temples indicate. These temples include: a temple of Hera, c530 B.C., known in later times

Temple of Hera (Basilica), c530 B.C.
Mary E. Dolbeare

as the Basilica; a temple of Athena, c510 B.C., known later as temple of Ceres; a temple dedicated to Hera, c450 B.C., but later called the temple of Poseidon. Each of these temples preserves its peristyles, or outer colonnades, intact, and the temple of Poseidon (Hera) further preserves its interior supports, small Doric columns in two stories. Excavations of two more temples of Hera at the mouth of the river Silarus (Sele), five miles to the north, have produced delightful sculptured metopes in the archaic style that are now displayed in the Paestum museum. Together, these temples form an outstanding gallery of Doric architecture, surpassed in impressiveness and wealth of information only by the Periclean buildings of Athens. Yet

153

Temple of Poseidon, c450 B.C.
Mary E. Dolbeare

Temple of Poseidon, Columns
Mary E. Dolbeare

(obscured) errạnt, ardẹnt, actọr; ch, chip; g, go; th, thin; ŦH, then; y, you; (variable) ḍ as d or j, ṣ as s or sh, ṭ as t or ch, ẓ as z or zh.

no ancient writer ever happened to mention them. Beginning about 400 B.C. native Italian tribes, the Lucani, attacked Posidonia and soon gained control of the city, whose inhabitants they are said to have oppressed. The greater part of the city fortifications, two and a half miles in circuit and still preserved throughout their entire length, appears to be of Greek construction, with extensive repairs attributed to the Lucanians. Four main gates survive, as well as a number of posterns and sally ports, some blocked up, and many towers. Of these towers, those later adapted for use as farm buildings have survived almost intact. From this period date also a number of painted Lucanian tombs. After the collapse (275 B.C.) of Pyrrhus' invasion of Italy, Posidonia fell under the domination of the Romans, who established there (273 B.C.) a Latin colony under the name of Paestum, the name by which it is now usually known (Italian, Pesto). To the period of Roman domination belong new temples, an amphitheater, houses, and paved streets. Under the Empire, however, malaria increased and the population declined. To this circumstance we must credit the partial survival of the three great temples and the superb fortifications, which a more vigorous population would surely have dismantled to obtain their stones for building material. The temple of Athena (known as the temple of Ceres) became a church, and still contains traces of Christian tombs, but after a destructive Saracen raid in the 9th century the site was deserted. Paestum's temples remained unknown to western scholarship until 1745, when the Italian traveler Antonini described them. Recent excavations by Claudio Pellegrino Sestieri have revealed streets, Roman houses, fresh data on the history of the fortifications, painted tombs, and an extraordinary underground ritual chamber containing a bed and jars of offerings. (JJ)

Painted Portico or Colonnade. [Also: ***Stoa Poikile.***] A portico in the market-place, at Athens, founded by Pisianax. The walls of the portico were covered with paintings. One of the pictures showed the Athenians arrayed against the Spartans at Oenoë in Argolis, the date of which incident is unknown. Another, by Micon of Athens, was of Theseus fighting the Amazons. A third, by Polygnotus, showed the Greeks victorious at Troy gathered in an assembly to consider the outraging of Cassandra by Ajax the Lesser; and a fourth, by Micon and Panaenus, portrayed the fighting at the Battle of Marathon, in which were portraits of Callimachus the polemarch and Miltiades. Pausanias the traveler saw the paintings in the 2nd century A.D., but by the end of the 4th century they had disappeared. The Athenians dedicated the shields they had taken from the Spartans on the island of Sphacteria in 425 B.C. in the Painted Portico, and covered them with pitch so that they would not rust. Zeno, the philosopher, walked with his disciples in the Painted Portico, and discussed philosophy with them, whence came their name Stoics, from the *stoa* (colonnade, or portico), in which they developed their principles.

Pamphilus (pam'fi-lus). Greek painter of the first half of the 4th century B.C. He came from Macedonia and worked chiefly at Sicyon, as a teacher in the school founded there by Eupompus. Among his pupils was Apelles. He was the first to base the teaching of art on scientific principles, maintaining that painters had to have a knowledge of arithmetic and geometry in order to perfect their art. He is also said to have been responsible for introducing drawing as a school subject in Sicyon.

Panaenus (pa̧-nē'nus). Greek painter, active about the middle of the 5th century B.C. He was a brother or a nephew of Phidias, and worked with him on the great statue of Zeus at Olympia, of which, some say, Panaenus painted the drapery. He also worked with Micon on the painting of the *Battle of Marathon* in the Painted

(obscured) errant, ardent, actor; ch, chip; g, go; th, thin; ᴛʜ, then; y, you; (variable) d̠ as d or j, s̠ as s or sh, t̠ as t or ch, z̠ as z or zh.

Portico at Athens, a decoration now lost.

Panaetius (pạ-nē'shi-us) **Painter.** See **Euphronius,** painter and potter.

Parrhasius (pạ-rā'shi-us). Greek painter, considered one of the greatest of antiquity. He was born at Ephesus and was active in Athens, c400 B.C., as one of the chief representatives of the Ionic school. He was said to have had a painting contest with Zeuxis, another leading painter of the Ionic school. Zeuxis painted a bunch of grapes, which so deceived the birds that they swooped down and pecked at them. But Parrhasius painted a curtain which deceived Zeuxis himself, and won the contest. The anecdotes of Pliny about all the painters of this time indicate extraordinary realism carried to the point of actual illusion, as in the above case. There were many pen-and-ink sketches by Parrhasius still in existence in the time of Pliny. Among his principal works were *The Personification of the Demos of Athens,* probably suggested by Aristophanes, in which he portrayed great variety of psychological expressions in depicting the many types that made up the Athenian people; a *Prometheus;* the *Heracles* at Lindus; the *Theseus* at Athens, afterward on the Capital at Rome; a *Contest of Ajax and Odysseus for the Arms of Achilles;* and a *Madness of Odysseus.* He was one of the first to observe and utilize the proportions in human anatomy, and was skilled in the use of delicate coloring, as well as interested in catching rather violent activity in facial expressions.

Parthenon (pär'thẹ-non). The popular name for the splendid marble Doric temple of Athena Polias (Athena of the City), built on the Acropolis of Athens, between 447 and 438 B.C. It represents the peak achievement of Greek architecture. It was the third of three temples of Athena on this site. The first was a modest Doric temple of the limestone known as poros, restored with tristyle-in-antis porches at front and rear, the so-called Hecatompedon or "100-foot" temple. The foundations of this temple, buried beneath the later Parthenons, cannot be seen, but its dimensions and plan can be deduced from elements of the entablature and pediments which have survived, and which indicate a date somewhat earlier than 550 B.C., in the time of the Pisistratids.

In the wave of enthusiasm which followed the repulse of the Persians at Marathon in 490 B.C., the Hecatompedon was deliberately demolished to make place for the second temple, a more pretentious structure. This was the "Older Parthenon," designed as a hexastyle Doric temple, of marble from the quarries then recently opened on Mount Pentelicus, and was the first large construction in Pentelic marble. When the Persians, returning in 480 B.C., captured and burned Athens, the Older Parthenon was in scaffolding; construction had proceeded only as far as the limestone platform, the steps, and, to a height of from two to four drums each, the columns of the peristyle. In the fire these were badly damaged. Before the battle of Plataea (479 B.C.), the Greek allies had sworn not to rebuild the sanctuaries which had been burned and thrown down by the Persians, but to leave them in perpetuity as memorials of barbarian impiety. In accordance with this, the older Parthenon stood in ruin for 30 years; but in 449 B.C. Pericles annulled the oath, and ordered plans drawn up for the most magnificent temple yet seen. The architects were Ictinus and Callicrates, the sculptor in charge was Phidias. They designed an octastyle Doric temple, of Pentelic marble, with 17 columns on the flanks, measuring 101 by 228 feet on the top of the stylobate. Within the peristyle, two steps up from the stylobate, was the cella, itself divided into two chambers, the cella proper, called the *Hecatompedon*, in which was the cult statue, and a rear room called the *Parthenon*, the chamber of the Virgin (*parthenos*, "virgin"), each approached through a hexastyle portico. The cella had interior supports in the

(obscured) errant, ardent, actor; ch, chip; g, go; th, thin; ᴛʜ, then; y, you; (variable) ḍ as d or j, ṣ as s or sh, ṭ as t or ch, ẓ as z or zh.

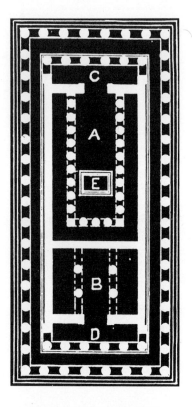

PLAN OF THE PARTHENON
A) cella; B) opisthodomus (or Parthenon); C) pronaos; D)
epinaos (or opisthodomus); E) site of the statue of Athena

form of small Doric columns in two stories, the Parthenon in the form of four tall, slender, Ionic columns.
The sculptured decorations, designed by Phidias and
executed under his supervision, the finest architectural
sculpture created in the Greek world, consisted of the
east and west pediments, a Doric frieze of 92 metopes,
and an Ionic frieze in low relief which ran completely
around the naos within the peristyle, at the top of the
cella wall and above the columns of the vestibules. The
east pediment represented the birth of Athena, when
Hephaestus split Zeus' aching head open with an ax.

159

Parthenon, NW view, 438 B.C.
Greek National Tourist Office

(obscured) errant, ardent, actor; ch, chip; g, go; th, thin; ᵵн, then; y, you;
(variable) ḍ as d or j, ş as s or sh, ţ as t or ch, ẓ as z or zh.

The west pediment represented the contest between Athena and Poseidon for chief place in the worship of the Athenians. The 92 metopes of the Doric frieze carried scenes in high relief of the battles of gods and giants on the east front, centaurs and Lapiths on the south, Amazons and Athenians on the west, and the fall of Troy on the north. The superb Ionic frieze, 523 feet in length, represented the Panathenaic procession of officials, youth and maidens, and sacrificial animals,

Parthenon, W front, 438 B.C.
Lillian Travis

that was the high point of the great festival of Athena held every four years. Phidias himself executed the gold and ivory (chryselephantine) cult statue of Athena, tinted ivory for the face and throat, arms, and feet, and gold for the clothing, armor, and attributes, 42 feet in height. The staggering expenditure on the Parthenon and its brilliant decorations was severely criticized by those who opposed governmental extravagance in any form, by those who were a little

fat, fāte, fär, fåll, åsk, fāre; net, mē, hėr; pin, pīne; not, nōte, möve, nôr; up, lūte, půll; oi, oil; ou out; (lightened) ẹlect, agǫny, ụnite;

EQUESTRIAN GROUP
From the W frieze of the Parthenon
British Museum

(obscured) errant, ardent, actor; ch, chip; g, go; th, thin; ŦH, then; y, you;
(variable) ḍ as d or j, ṣ as s or sh, ṭ as t or ch, ẓ as z or zh.

sensitive about the source of the funds, which Athens had blandly diverted to its own purposes from the reserves of the Delian Confederacy, and by those who hoped to profit by discrediting or embarrassing Pericles. Even after the dedication some residue of bitterness found expression in the litigation traditionally so dear to Athenian hearts. Phidias, for instance, was accused of having converted to his personal advantage some of the gold for the cult statue with which he had

LAPITH FIGHTING WITH A CENTAUR
Metope from S face of the Parthenon
British Museum

been entrusted, but refuted the charge by revealing that he had cast the gold in artfully fitted plates which could be dismantled, verified by weighing, and reassembled. Again, he was accused of impiety in that among the figures in the scene of the battle of Marathon, on Athena's shield, he had included recognizable portraits of himself and Pericles. Whatever the validity of the charge, it is known that Phidias left Athens and lived in exile for some years.

When its service to the pagan goddess was completed, the Parthenon was converted into a church of the Theotokos, the Mother of God. In 1204 (or 1208 A.D.) the Frankish Dukes of Athens turned it over to Rome. About 1460, after the Turkish conquest, it became a mosque. In 1687, during a siege of Athens by the Venetians under Morosini, a Venetian cannon ball exploded gunpowder stored in the mosque by the Turks, destroying the cella, the pronaos, 14 columns of the peristyle, and the mosque; afterward the Turks built a smaller mosque amid the wreckage. In 1801–3 Lord Elgin removed a great number of "architectural marbles," and as the Elgin Marbles they are among the chief treasures of the British Museum. These include 18 figures from the pediments, almost half of the frieze, and 15 metopes. Those sculptures which remain in place on the Parthenon have suffered grievously from weathering. Dominating the whole city from its position on the highest eminence of the Acropolis, of the golden rust color characteristic of weathered Pentelic marble, the Parthenon has survived age, wars, and changing times as a memorial to that surge of intellectual and artistic grandeur which we know as the Golden Age of Pericles. (JJ)

Pasiteles (pa̱-sit′e̱-lēz). Greek sculptor, a native of Magna Graecia, of the 1st century B.C. He acquired Roman citizenship (c87 B.C.) when the southern cities were admitted to that privilege. He followed the modern method of elaborating his work in clay, and wrote five books on artistic matters much quoted by Pliny. Pasiteles and his school affected a kind of pre-Phidian style. Many pseudo-archaic works are ascribed to them.

Pausias (pô'si-as, -shi-). Greek painter of Sicyon, active in the middle of the 4th century B.C. He was a pupil of Pamphilus and a contemporary of Apelles. He made a special study of foreshortening, and was the first to paint ceiling-panels. A famous picture was the *Stephanoplocus* or *Stephanopolis*, painted from Glycera, a flower girl of Sicyon. He painted *Love*, without his bow and arrows and carrying a lyre, in the Tholos (*Round House*) at Epidaurus, and also a picture of *Drunkenness* staring at himself from the bottom of his cup. He was especially attracted by the possibilities of encaustic (the technique of using heated wax to apply colors on stone or wood), and developed it to a high degree of perfection.

Pediment (ped'i-ment). In classical architecture, a low triangular part resembling a gable, crowning the fronts of temples, especially over porticos. It was surrounded by a cornice and its flat recessed field was often ornamented with sculptures in relief or in the round. Some of the most beautiful and important examples of Greek sculpture come from temple pediments, as those from the Temple of Aphaea, Aegina, now in the Glyptotek, Munich, from the Parthenon, Acropolis Museum and British Museum, and from the Temple of Zeus at Olympia, now in the Olympia Museum.

Pelike (pel'i-kē). In ancient Greece, a large vase resembling the hydria, but with the curve between the neck and the body less marked, and having only two handles, attached to the neck at or near the rim and extending to the body.

Pergamum (pėr'ga-mum). [Also: *Pergamus;* modern name, *Bergama*.] The word appears to mean "citadel" or "stronghold." In ancient geography, a city in Mysia, Asia Minor, about 50 miles N of Smyrna. The city was raised to importance by the famous victory of Attalus I over the Gauls in the latter half of the 3rd century B.C. Attalus I celebrated this victory by dedicating a series of bronze statues on the acropolis of Pergamum, and

fat, fāte, fär, fåll, åsk, fãre; net, mē, hėr; pin, pīne; not, nōte, möve, nôr; up, lūte, pûll; oi, oil; ou out; (lightened) ẹlect, agǫny, ụnite;

later a second series at Athens. Of some of these statues marble copies survive: *The Dying Gaul* in the
Capitoline Museum, Rome; the *Ludovisi Gaul,* and the
head of the *Dying Asiatic,* in the National Museum
(Museo delle Terme), Rome; another *Dying Gaul* and
Dying Asiatic, and a *Dead Amazon,* in the National Museum, Naples; and others elsewhere. To the son of
Attalus, Eumenes II, are due the great extension of the
city as well as its architectural adornment, and during
his reign occurred the remarkable development of Pergamene sculpture, on lines much more modern in
spirit than the older Greek art. The same king founded
a famous library here. His chief buildings were placed
on a succession of terraces on the summit of the
acropolis, which rises 900 feet above the plain, and on
the other lower terraces immediately outside the powerful acropolis walls. The city remained prosperous
under the Romans, and under the empire many fine
buildings were erected on the acropolis, and beside
the river below. In 1878 the Prussian government sent
to the site an exploring expedition under Alexander
Conze and Karl Humann. Their investigations were
continued for several years, and to them are due the
rediscovery of Pergamene art and the mass of information regarding later Greek architecture which together
form one of the most remarkable archaeological acqui-
sitions of that century. There are also a Greek theater,
a Roman amphitheater, and remains of several temples. An Ionic temple of the finest Greek design is on
the slope of the acropolis; the cella with its ornamented doorway remains unusually perfect. The temple of Athena Polias, a Doric peripteros of six by ten
columns, of late Greek date, measuring 42½ by 72
feet, occupied a terrace surrounded on two or three
sides by a handsome stoa of two stories, Doric below
and Ionic above, with a balustrade sculptured with
warlike trophies in the second story. The Great Altar
of Zeus, with its high-relief sculptures of the *Battle of*

(obscured) errạnt, ardẹnt, actọr; ch, chip; g, go; th, thin; ŦH, then; y, you;
(variable) ḍ as d or j, ṣ as s or sh, ṭ as t or ch, ẓ as z or zh.

Gods and Giants, is one of the landmarks of Hellenistic art. The continuous frieze is seven feet high and 400 feet long. The temple of Trajan, occupying a large terrace toward the summit of the acropolis, was a Corinthian peripteros of white marble.

Peribolus (pe-rib′ō-lus). In Greek antiquity, a consecrated court or inclosure, generally surrounded by a wall, and often containing a temple, statues, etc.

Periclean (per-i-klē′ạn) *Architecture.* A classification under which are listed a number of marble temples and other buildings erected in Attica during the intellectual and aesthetic hegemony of Pericles. The period of Periclean architecture began with the eclipse of Cimon and Ephialtes in 461 B.C. and survived the death of Pericles (429 B.C.). At Pericles' instigation and under his close supervision, Athens embarked on a broad program of civic embellishment. A partial list of Periclean buildings, with their locations, style, architects, and approximate dates, follows: Temple of Hephaestus, formerly called the Theseum (Athens; Doric; the Theseum architect (q.v.); c449–c444B.C.); Temple on the Ilissus (Athens; Ionic; Callicrates; c449 B.C.); Hall of the Mysteries (Eleusis; Doric; Ictinus and others; c450 B.C.); Parthenon (Athens; Doric; Ictinus and Callicrates; begun 447 B.C., dedicated 438 B.C.); Odeum of Pericles (Athens; architect unknown; after 450 B.C.?); Temple of Poseidon (Sunium; Doric; the Theseum architect; c444–c440 B.C.); Temple of Ares (Athens; Doric; the Theseum architect; c440–c436 B.C.); Propylaea (Athens; Doric; Mnesicles; c437–c432 B.C.); Temple of Nemesis (Rhamnus; Doric; the Theseum architect; c436–c432 B.C.). Buildings begun after Pericles' death continued the traditions he established: Temple of Athena Nike (Athens; Ionic; architect unknown, possibly Mnesicles; begun 421, finished 405 B.C.); Stoa of Zeus (Athens; Doric; architect unknown; last quarter of the 5th century B.C.). To this list may properly be added temples outside of Attica, by architects in the Periclean tradition: Temple of Apollo (Bassae; Doric; Ictinus; c450–c425 B.C.); Temple of Apollo (Delos; Doric; architect unknown; c425 B.C.). (JJ)

Peripteros (pẹ-rip′tẹ-ros). A temple of which the cella is surrounded by a single range of columns.

Peristyle (per′i-stīl). In architecture, a range or ranges of columns surrounding any part, as the cella of a Greek temple, or any place, as a court or cloister, or the atrium of a classical house.

Phaestus (fes′tus). [Also: *Phaistos.*] In ancient geography, a city of Crete, situated in the middle of the south side of the island, on a hill 300 feet above the plain of Mesara. To the N and W, Cretan Mount Ida, where some say Zeus was born, rises above the plain. The city is mentioned by Homer in the *Iliad* as one which sent men against Troy under the leadership of Idomeneus. It was one of the most ancient cities of Crete. According to legend it was founded by Minos, whose nephew Gortys, son of Rhadamanthys, later destroyed the citadel and added the area to his realm. Remains at the site show that there were three distinct periods of occupation. The first structures date from the neolithic age. In the second period, c2000 B.C., a palace was built on the site, remains of which indicate a highly developed and prosperous civilization. This palace was destroyed, or partly destroyed, c1700 B.C., by some catastrophe, either by earthquake, or by enemy raids. However, the interruption in the prosperity of Phaestus was temporary, and a second and larger palace was constructed on the ruins of the first. This too was destroyed by means unknown, c1400 B.C.; after this the site was relatively unoccupied and was ultimately crowned by a temple of the classical period. Among present remains are traces of the structures of all three periods. Work on the excavation of the site, begun in 1900 by the Italians under Federigo Halbherr and continued in subsequent years, is still proceeding. The palace, which lies on terraces of differing levels connected by large and small staircases, follows the general plan of that at Cnossus but on a smaller scale and with more refinement. The general plan of the installations on the site includes a large paved court where dances and games were held, a theater, rooms for the performance of sacrifices, with channels to collect the blood of victims, gypsum shelves for the exhibition of statues and cult objects, an ingenious system for supplying the area with water and an intricate drainage system. The palace itself, approached through a propylaeum, had a large central court with porticoes, at least on the east and west sides, a great colonnaded reception hall that was approached by a majestic stairway, *megaron* (central hall), guest rooms, baths, storage areas, and other chambers for the use of the royal family and those occupied in serving it. The women's quarters were separate from the men's. Only the king, by a private stairway, could pass the sentry who guarded the women's quarters. Remains of a bathroom and bath have been found. The bath was a sunken chamber, with steps leading down to it, surrounded by a balcony on which a maid might stand to pour water over her mistress. Some say, however, that such a sunken chamber had ceremonial significance, and was used for purification rites. As at Cnossus, careful and brilliant provision was made for insulating the palace against the hot sun of summer and the bitter winds that swept down from the north in winter. The plaster of the walls was mixed with straw to provide air spaces, even as is done today in the houses of the Cretan farmers. Two sets of doors, with an air space between them, protected the main chambers from drafts or heat. For light and ventilation the palace had light wells, covered at the top and with openings cut in the walls below the roof. Of the many finds at Phaestus, a clay disc that had been hardened and preserved in the fire that destroyed the palace was unique. On the

---

fat, fāte, fär, fåll, àsk, fãre; net, mē, hėr; pin, pīne; not, nōte, möve, nôr; up, lūte, pùll; oi, oil; ou out; (lightened) ēlect, agǫny, ūnite;

two faces of the Phaestus Disc appear pictographic inscriptions in spiral form, which, according to a recent effort at decipherment, can be read as Greek, and list Cretan shrines to be visited by the pious traveler.

Phiale (fī′a̱-lē). In ancient Greece, a flat, saucer-shaped vase used for pouring religious libations.

Phidias (fĭd′ĭ-as). Greek sculptor; the son of Charmides. He was born probably at Athens, c490 B.C.; died c430 B.C. He studied with Hegias of Athens, and later with Ageladas of Argos, who may have come to Athens in the time of Cimon. He became later, under Pericles, a counselor in political affairs at Athens as well as chief sculptor, and was a sort of supervisor of public works. Among his first works were 13 figures at Delphi ordered by Cimon, son of Miltiades, to commemorate the victory at Marathon, in which Miltiades was represented among gods and heroes. To this early period are ascribed also the *Athena Area* at Plataea, and the *Athena Promachus,* or bronze colossus, on the Acropolis at Athens. This figure was probably more than 30 feet high, and could be seen for a great distance. The statue, made in 460–450 B.C., was the largest ever made in Athens. The pedestal was discovered in 1845. The statue of *Olympian Zeus* at Elis, his greatest work and described by Pausanias, is supposed to have been about 42 feet high, seated and holding a Nike (Victory) in his hand. The flesh was of ivory and the drapery of gold, with inlaid or inscribed decoration. The throne itself, which rose above the head of the statue, was elaborately carved and decorated. Both throne and statue were surrounded with statues and paintings. Ancient writers also selected for special distinction his *Lemnian Athena,* dedicated c450 B.C. By 444 B.C. Phidias must have been at Athens, and intimately associated with Pericles in his transformation of the city. All the great monuments of Athens, including the Parthenon, were erected at this time, within a period not longer than 20 years. The work of Phidias culminated in the

Athena Parthenos, a chryselephantine (gold and ivory) statue of Athena in the cella of the Parthenon. It was finished and consecrated in 438 B.C. The figure was about 38 feet high, standing, and held a Nike in her right hand. The *Varvakeion Athena* at Athens (discovered in 1881) represents the statue, but inadequately. The enormous expense of these works, which was paid with money exacted from the allies of Athens, brought both Pericles and Phidias into difficulties. According to Plutarch, Phidias was accused of appropriating the gold devoted to the statue to his own use. The gold was removed, weighed, and found to be intact. He was then accused of sacrilege in representing Pericles and himself on the shield of the goddess. In one version he was condemned, thrown into prison, and died there, possibly of poison. The actual style of Phidias is best represented in the well-known fragments of the frieze of the Parthenon. Among the independent statues by Phidias was an *Amazon* at Ephesus which took second prize in competition with Polyclitus. This is supposed to be represented by the *Amazon Mattei* of the Vatican.

Phigalian Marbles (fi-gā'li-an). See *Bassae.*

Philo (fī'lō). Greek sculptor of the time of Alexander the Great. Among his works was a statue of Alexander's friend Hephaestion and an image of Zeus that was set up at the entrance to the Bosporus.

Philo. Athenian architect; fl. latter part of the 4th century B.C. He built the portico to the great temple at Eleusis for Demetrius Phalereus (c318 B.C.), and ship installations at the Piraeus. The latter were destroyed by Sulla (86 B.C.).

Phintias (fin'ti-as). Attic potter and painter, active at the end of the 6th and the beginning of the 5th centuries B.C. His signature as painter appears on four extant vessels, as potter on three. A cup (Munich), c520 B.C., is inscribed "Deiniades made, Phintias painted." The inside of the cup has a Silen with a drinking cup. One side of the outside shows Heracles and Apollo struggling for the Olympic tripod; the other side shows Heracles slaying the giant Alcyoneus, as Hermes watches. The decoration is executed in the red-figure style. A hydria (Munich) c510 B.C., also in red-figure style, shows a music lesson, and on the shoulder, two hetairai playing the game of cottabus.

Phryne (frī'nē). [Original name, **Mnesarete.**] Boeotia-born, 4th century B.C. Athenian courtesan. She is supposed to have been the model of the picture *Aphrodite Anadyomene* by Apelles, and of the statue of the Cnidian Aphrodite by Praxiteles. According to legend, she was defended on a capital charge by her lover Hyperides; and when he failed to move the judges by his oratory, he bade her uncover her bosom, after which they voted her acquittal.

Piraeus (pī-rē'us). [Also: **Peiraeus, Peiraieus, Peiraievs, Piraieus.**] Seaport of Athens and the chief port of Greece, situated on the Saronic Gulf about 5 miles SW of Athens, on the west side of the Munychian peninsula. The ancients believed the Piraeus was once an island, and its name is taken to mean "land across the water." Themistocles recognized the advantages of Piraeus, with its three harbors, over Phalerum, Athens' ancient port, and during his archonship (493–492 B.C.) he fortified the Piraeus and built it up as a port. In c450 B.C. Hippodamus of Miletus remodeled the city, laying out the streets in squares or rectangles, the so-called grid-iron system. The great ship sheds there were one of the glories of Athens. Among the artifacts found on the site of the ship sheds are marble plates, with a great eye painted on them. These plates were fastened to the bows of the ships, providing an eye so that the ship could see where it was going. The port was connected to Athens by long walls, and ultimately this whole area was enclosed in a single fortification. At the end of the Peloponnesian Wars (404 B.C.), the Spartans destroyed the fortifications. They were rebuilt in 394 B.C. by Conon, who also founded a sanctuary of Aphrodite near the SE rim of the great harbor. Sulla destroyed the fortifications (c86 B.C.) and they were never rebuilt. At the Piraeus there was a sacred precinct of Athena Savior with a bronze image of the goddess holding a spear; and there was a precinct of Zeus Savior with a bronze image of the god holding a staff and Victory. Themistocles founded a sanctuary of Aphrodite at the NE extremity of the Piraeus. There were, among other religious sites, at least two theaters of Dionysus there. In 1959 it was reported that a cache of ancient statues had been discovered at Piraeus by workmen digging during street repairs. From the charring of the walls of the chamber in which the statues were found and the fact that the statues are of various ages, archaeologists have conjectured that the statues had been collected in a warehouse and then abandoned after a fire there, possibly in the 1st century B.C. The most notable of the statues is the Apollo, a bronze figure of excellent workmanship that dates from the last quarter of the 6th century B.C. It is probably the oldest full-size bronze figure in the world. Several statues dating from the 4th century B.C. were found; these include a bronze female figure, a marble statue of a maiden, a five-foot-high bronze statue of Artemis, and an eight-foot-high bronze of Athena, her helmet etched with intricate designs. Several hermae of marble and bronze, thought to be 1st century B.C. Roman copies, were also found there.

Pistoxenus (pis-toks′ẹ-nus) *Painter.* See *Euphronius,* painter and potter.

Plato (plā′tō). Greek bust in bronze, of the first half of the 4th century B.C., in the Museo Nazionale, Naples, once supposed to represent the great philosopher. Many consider it a bearded type of Dionysus; some, the famous Poseidon of Tarentum.

Polyclitus (pol-i-klī′tus) or *Polycletus* (-klē′tus). [Sometimes called *Polyclitus of Sicyon;* also known as *Polyclitus the Elder.*] Greek sculptor and architect in the last

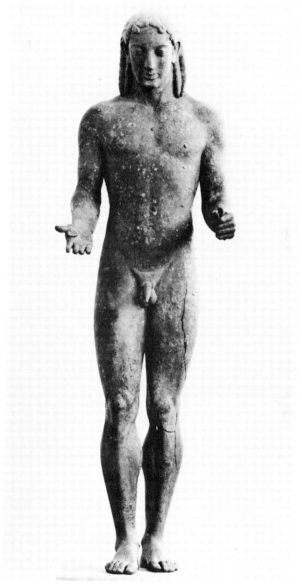

APOLLO
Bronze, 6th century B.C., found at Piraeus
National Museum, Athens
T.A.P. Service

(obscured) errant, ardent, actor; ch, chip; g, go; th, thin; ŦH, then; y, you;
(variable) ḍ as d or j, ṣ as s or sh, ṭ as t or ch, ẓ as z or zh.

half of the 5th century B.C., an older contemporary of
Phidias. He is associated with the high development of
abstract proportion which characterizes Greek sculpture. He seems to have realized the athletic type of
ideal to the entire satisfaction of the Greek world, and
made a figure embodying the accepted proportions,
which was called "the canon." This canon is supposed
to have been a simple figure carrying a spear *(doryphorus)*, described by Pliny and now represented by
several copies. The best of these was found at Pompeii,
and is in the museum at Naples. Another statue of
almost equal importance is mentioned by Pliny, and
called *diadumenus* (i.e., an athlete binding a fillet about
his head). The best copy is in the British Museum. The
most important monumental work of Polyclitus was
the chryselephantine Hera at Argos, which has completely disappeared; representations of it are found on
coins. An Amazon Polyclitus made for Ephesus, also
lost, was considered by the ancients to be the equal, if
not the superior, of the Amazon of Phidias. In general,
Polyclitus worked in bronze, and confined himself to
statues of athletic victors.

Polyclitus the Younger. Greek sculptor of Argos; fl. c400
B.C.

Polydorus (pol-i-dō′rus). Rhodian sculptor, associate of
Agesander in carving the Laocoön group.

Polygnotus (pol-ig-nō′tus). Greek painter, born on the
island of Thasus. He was active in Athens c475–447
B.C. He was identified with Cimon in the reconstruction of Athens, and seems to have had about him a
large school or force of assistants. In recognition of his
merit as an artist he was given Athenian citizenship. He
worked on the Painted Portico in Athens, where a picture of *The Capture of Troy* was attributed to him. In this
picture Elpinice, sister of Cimon, appeared as Laodice,
daughter of King Priam. Among his other known
works was the *Marriage of the Dioscuri to the Leucippides* in
the sanctuary of the Dioscuri at Athens, and very cele-

fat, fāte, fär, fȧll, ȧsk, fâre; net, mē, hėr; pin, pīne; not, nōte, mȯve,
nôr; up, lūte, ṗull; oi, oil; ou out; (lightened) ẹlect, agọny, ụnite;

brated paintings of the *Capture of Troy* and the *Descent of Odysseus into Hades* at Delphi. Polygnotus introduced transparent draperies and many realistic effects; for example, Pausanias tells that a hare in the picture of the marriage of the Dioscuri was greatly admired for its lifelike effect.

Porinus (pō-rī'nus). Sixth century B.C. Greek architect, associated with Antistates, Antimachides, and Callaeschrus in preparing the original plans for the Olympieum, the colossal temple of Zeus Olympius at Athens projected by the Pisistratids. (JJ)

Praxiteles (prak-sit'ę-lēz). Greek sculptor, born at Athens about the end of the 5th century B.C. He was the son of the sculptor Cephisiodotus, and was a younger contemporary of Scopas. His activity lasted until about the time of Alexander the Great, or 336 B.C. Nearly threescore of his works are mentioned in old writers. The characteristics of his work—relaxed and graceful strength, extraordinary modeling and delicate contours—are shown in the statue of *Hermes Carrying the Infant Dionysus*, identified by Pausanias' description, and found at Olympia in 1877. Of the many works described with admiration and enthusiasm by the ancient writers, the *Hermes* and three heads are the only surviving originals of Praxiteles. Various works in modern museums are copies of his work. Among them is the *Satyr* of the Capitol in Rome (the *Marble Faun* of Hawthorne's novel). Of this there is a story that Phryne, a courtesan who sometimes served as the model for Praxiteles, once asked him to give her the most beautiful of his works. Loverlike, as Pausanias says, he agreed to do so, but couldn't say which he thought was most beautiful. She sent a slave to give him the alarm that fire had broken out in his studio. Praxiteles rushed to the studio, crying that his work was all wasted if fire had destroyed his *Satyr* and his *Eros*. Having found out what he most valued, Phryne chose to take the statue of *Eros*. The original *Satyr* was

(obscured) errạnt, ardẹnt, actọr; ch, chip; g, go; th, thin; ŦH, then; y, you;
(variable) ḍ as d or j, ş as s or sh, ṭ as t or ch, ẓ as z or zh.

in a temple of Dionysus at Athens. Other copies of his work are a beautiful torso discovered in the Palatine, and now in the Louvre; the *Apollino* of the tribune in Florence; and the *Apollo Sauroctonus* (Lizard-slayer) of

PRAXITELES
Hermes Carrying the Infant Dionysus
German Archaeological Museum, Athens

fat, fāte, fär, fåll, åsk, fãre; net, mē, hėr; pin, pīne; not, nōte, möve, nôr; up, lūte, pùll; oi, oil; ou out; (lightened) ẹlect, agọny, ụnite;

the Vatican. His most celebrated work was the *Aphrodite of Cnidus,* which, next to the *Zeus* of Phidias, was the most admired of the statues of antiquity. Of the *Aphrodite,* it is said that Praxiteles was commissioned to exe-

PRAXITELES
Detail

cute a statue of Aphrodite for the Athenians. He made two, one of which was a nude, the first time the female figure had been sculptured without drapery. The

Athenians considered the two statues and chose the more conventional draped one. The Cnidians eagerly purchased the nude. This is the statue that came to be known as the *Aphrodite of Cnidus.*

Prochoös (prō′kō̱-os). In Greek antiquity, a small vase of elegant form, resembling the oinochoë, but in general more slender, and with a handle rising higher above the rim: used especially to pour water on the hands before meals were served (and also to pour from for libations).

Pronaos (prō̱-nā′os). An open vestibule or portico in front of the naos or cella of a Greek temple.

Propylaea (prop-i-lē′ạ). Monumental gateway to the Acropolis at Athens, begun 437 B.C. by Mnesicles. It consists of a central ornamented passage and two projecting wings, that on the N with a chamber (the Pinacotheca) behind its small portico. The central passage has on both W and E faces a magnificent hexastyle Doric portico. At about two thirds of its length it is crossed by a wall pierced with five doorways, the widest and highest in the middle. An inclined way passes through the wider middle intercolumniations of both great porches and the large central door; this way was flanked between the W portico and the door by six tall Ionic columns, whose capitals supply the most beautiful type of the order.

Propylaeum (prop-i-lē′um). An important architectural vestibule or entrance to a sacred inclosure or other precinct, as that of the Acropolis of Athens, or that of the sanctuary of Eleusis; usually in the plural: *propylaea.* In its origin it was a strongly fortified gateway, but it became developed into an ornamental structure, often elaborate and magnificent, with which were combined gates of more or less defensive strength.

Protogenes (prō̱-toj′ẹ-nēz). Greek painter; born at Caunus, in Caria, Asia Minor (or at Xanthus in Lycia); fl. in the second half of the 4th century B.C. He spent most of his life at Rhodes. He was noted for the care

fat, fāte, fär, fȧll, ȧsk, fāre; net, mē, hėr; pin, pīne; not, nōte, möve, nôr; up, lūte, pu̇ll; oi, oil; ou out; (lightened) ẹlect, agọny, ụnite;

and time he spent on each of his paintings, and is said to have put four layers of paint on some of his works so that if the first layer wore off the next would replace it. Among his most famous works was the *Ialysus,* of which the subject was the hero who founded the town that bore his name on Rhodes. Protogenes is said to have spent seven years in completing the picture. It was at Rhodes for at least 200 years, then was carried off to Rome and placed in the Temple of Peace, where it perished when the temple was destroyed by fire. Another of his famous works was the *Resting Satyr* on which he worked at Rhodes all during the siege of the city by Demetrius Poliorcetes (305–304 B.C.), regardless that the garden in which he worked was in the midst of the enemy camp. It is said that Demetrius, on learning of the artist's presence, took measures to protect him and his work. He also had paintings in the Propylaea and the Bouleterium at Athens. It is said that Protogenes was a poor and self-taught man, whose great skill and art went unrecognized until Apelles, his great contemporary, publicly and generously expressed his admiration for them.

Psiax (sī′aks). Attic vase-painter, active c520 B.C. Formerly called the Menon Painter, from an amphora (Philadelphia) made by the potter Menon, he was later identified by two vases signed by him as painter and by Hilinus as potter. Twenty-eight other vessels have been attributed to him. With the Andocides Painter, he was one of the earliest to use the red-figure style. Active when this style was beginning to replace black-figure, he worked in both, and sometimes used both on the same vessel.

Psykter (sik′tẻr). A type of Greek vase used for cooling wine. The body is of conoid form, with short cylindrical neck and a somewhat tall cylindrical foot, adapted in form for insertion in the crater, and for standing on the table. It was sometimes supported on a tripod.

Pylus (pī′lus). In ancient geography, a town in N Mes-

(obscured) errᶏnt, ardᶒnt, actǫr; ch, chip; g, go; th, thin; ᴛʜ, then; y, you;
(variable) ḍ as d or j, ṣ as s or sh, ṭ as t or ch, ᵶ as z or zh.

senia, Greece, situated N and E of the Gulf of Navarino. The "sandy Pylus" of the *Iliad* and the *Odyssey*, it was about two and a half miles from the Bay of Pylus. (The bay has since been converted into a lagoon

PSYKTER
Red-figured, 5th century B.C.

by a sandbar that blocks its mouth.) According to legend, this Pylus was founded by Pylas, who came into the region from Megara and whose companions were Leleges. It later fell into the hands of Neleus, who raised the city to such renown that Homer called it "the city of Neleus," and later into the hands of his son Nestor. In ancient times Pylus was a place of considerable importance. Nestor's palace was the peer, in size and wealth, of the palace of Agamemnon at Mycenae. Until 1939 the location of the palace of Nestor had been a matter of dispute; some placed it farther north, in Elis, and some placed it on the western promontory of the Gulf of Navarino that was known in ancient times as Coryphasium. In 1939 Prof. Carl W. Blegen, of the University of Cincinnati, located the palace of Nestor at Epano Englianos, a plateau about two and one-half miles from the modern village of Chora, when he and a Greek team uncovered the foundations and floor of the palace there. In 1952 and succeeding years, excavations under Prof. Blegen's direction have revealed the existence of a large palace dating from about 1300 B.C. Remains uncovered give a clear outline of the size and ground plan of the palace. Lying in a NW-SE direction on the plateau, the palace is roughly a huge rectangle that is divided lengthwise into three unequal parts. The central and largest portion is occupied, beginning at the SE end, by a portico, vestibule, great hall, and storage magazines. A narrow aisle on the southerly side has many small chambers. On the northerly side a wider aisle holds, from the southeast to the northeast, the queen's apartments, a bathroom, stairways to the upper floors, and more storage spaces. It is thought the palace had at least two stories, the walls of the first story being of soft limestone blocks, and those of the upper story being of crude brick. Fragments of pottery of all sizes and descriptions have been dug up. In one pantry alone, over 2800 drinking cups were found; these were shaped like champagne glasses, and the number of them was ascertained by counting the stems. The work of the excavators has revealed that the floors and walls of the palace were covered with plaster and decorated with paintings of dolphins, octopuses and other marine creatures, linear designs, floral patterns, winged griffins, and human figures in armor. The great hall, or throne room, was surrounded by an inside balcony from which the ladies, whose apartments were on the second floor, could observe the men. There was an intricate drainage system by which water from the roofs and terraces of the palace was collected and carried off by underground limestone conduits. A large, circular, decorated hearth was found in the throne

(obscured) errₐnt, ardᵉnt, actǫr; ch, chip; g, go; th, thin; ꞎH, then; y, you; (variable) ḍ as d or j, ṣ as s or sh, ṭ as t or ch, ẓ as z or zh.

room where, presumably, slices of bulls' thighs wrapped in fat were roasted when Nestor entertained. A smaller circular hearth was found in the queen's apartments. Fragments of terra-cotta chimney pots to carry off the smoke from the hearth fires have also been discovered. The remains of a bathroom, in which there was an unbroken tub, have also been found. In a wing connected to the palace by a kind of ramp, another tub has been located. A huge altar unearthed in a portico before this wing indicates that this area may have been the household shrine. One of the most important finds in the excavation of the palace was the discovery of what was apparently an archive room. In this were hundreds of clay tablets and fragments inscribed with the Linear Script B. These tablets were the first to be found on the mainland of Greece and prove that the Greeks had a written language at least as early as 1300 B.C. At the time the tablets were found the Linear Script B, so-named by Sir Arthur Evans who found it in Crete, had not been deciphered. It was at last deciphered in 1952. The inscriptions on the tablets list inventories of olive oil, wheat, figs, and other stores of the royal household, as well as accounts of work to be done and goods to be supplied to the palace. The palace was destroyed by fire, as indicated by the fused condition of the rocks, and the site was never again occupied, so that the outline of the original structure has not been confused by the remains of later buildings, as at Mycenae and Tiryns. In the neighborhood of the palace many tombs have been discovered, some of which have been excavated. In them were found swords with ivory handles, bits of gold leaf, small art objects, and other funerary offerings. Skulls have been found that may even be those of the heroes of Homer. The modern seaport of Pylos, on a promontory at the SE end of the Gulf of Navarino, is a town founded early in the 19th century. In the neighborhood is a vast cave, with oddly shaped rock formations.

This is said to be the cave where the cattle of Neleus and Nestor were kept. Because the sandy soil, whence its name "sandy Pylus," was unfit for growing grass, the cattle were driven to this area for grazing and were sheltered in this grotto. The modern Pylos has also been called *Navarino* and *Neocastro.*

Pythagoras (pi-thag′ọ̄-rạs, pī-). Greek sculptor, born in the island of Samos. He went to Rhegium, in Italy, where he was active in the first half of the 5th century B.C. He worked exclusively in bronze and rivaled his contemporaries, Polyclitus and Myron, in his statues of heroes and victors in the games. His statues, only one copy of which survives, were notable for lifelike play of the sinews and positions of the body.

Pyxis (pik′sis). In ancient Greece, a type of cylindrical vase or box with a cover, used especially by women, as for the toilet.

—R—

Rhodes (rōdz). [Greek: ***Rhodos, Rodos;*** Italian, ***Rodi;*** Latin, ***Rhodus.***] Island in the Aegean Sea, SW of Asia Minor and separated from the coast by a channel about seven miles wide. One of the Dodecanese Islands, it is about 45 miles long and about 545 square miles in area. The surface is mountainous and hilly. It is noted for its fertility and has an active commerce. The inhabitants are largely Greek. According to traditional accounts, Rhodes was first inhabited by the Telchines, who nursed the infant Poseidon there. When he grew up he fell in love with Halia, a sister of the Telchines, and by her had six sons and one daughter, Rhode or Rhodos. These six sons outraged the goddess Aphrodite and committed other evil deeds. To punish them, Aphrodite drove them mad, and Poseidon sank them under

(obscured) errạnt, ardẹnt, actọr; ch, chip; g, go; th, thin; ŦH, then; y, you;
(variable) ḍ as d or j, ṣ as s or sh, ṭ as t or ch, ẕ as z or zh.

the ground. Some say that when Zeus was parceling out the lands to the gods he absentmindedly forgot to award any to Helius, and when he thought of it, he was distressed. Helius offered to take an island that was just then rising from the great flood Zeus had sent over the world. Helius went there and found Poseidon's daughter Rhode, with whom he fell in love and for whom he named the island Rhodes. Thus, the island came to be known as "the Bride of the Sun." Rhodes is the scene of many myths and legends. Danaus, fleeing with his daughters from Egypt, stopped there and founded a temple of Athena at Lindus. Cadmus, searching for Europa, also touched at the island. He founded a temple to Poseidon in fulfillment of a vow he had made during a storm at sea, and also dedicated a bronze cauldron inscribed with Phoenician letters. According to some accounts, this was how the Phoenician alphabet was brought to the Greek world. Althaemenes, the son of Catreus of Crete, fled to Rhodes to escape an oracle that predicted he would kill his father. He built a temple to Zeus on Mount Atybrus, the highest point on the island, from which it was claimed he could see his beloved homeland. The flight of Althaemenes to Rhodes and his settlement there provide a legendary explanation for prehistoric colonization of the island by Cretans. Tlepolemus, the son of Heracles, also sought refuge on Rhodes, and became its king before he sailed to join Agamemnon in the war against Troy. His followers founded the three cities of Lindus, Camirus, and Ialysus and laid the legendary basis for the Dorian invasion of Rhodes about 1000 B.C. Some say that Helen, after the death of Menelaus, fled from Sparta because of the enmity with which she was regarded, and sought asylum in Rhodes with her former friend Polyxo, wife of Tlepolemus. But Polyxo now hated her because of the death of Tlepolemus in the Trojan War, and inspired her maids to hang Helen. At one time Rhodes was so infested by serpents that it

fat, fāte, fär, fâll, ȧsk, fāre; net, mē, hėr; pin, pīne; not, nōte, möve, nôr; up, lūte, pùll; oi, oil; ou out; (lightened) ĕlect, agǫny, ūnite;

was called "Ophidea." The inhabitants sent to the oracle of Apollo at Delphi for relief, and were told to admit Phorbas, son of Lapithes, to colonize the island. The Rhodians sent for Phorbas, who came with his companions and destroyed the serpents. After his death he was accorded a hero's honors by the grateful people. Some say the three chief cities of the island—Ialysus, Lindus, and Camirus—were named for three daughters of Danaus who died there. Others say they were named for three grandsons of Helius, and that they founded the cities after a great flood and divided the island into three parts, each of the cities being the center of the area which each of the brothers ruled.

In prehistoric times Rhodes was colonized by Phoenicians and Cretans, and later by Dorians, and its three cities formed, with Halicarnassus, Cnidus, and Cos, the "Dorian Hexapolis." At the beginning of the 6th century B.C. the island fell under the domination of the Persians. After the Persian War it joined the first Athenian Confederacy, 478 B.C., from which it withdrew by revolt at the end of the 5th century. In 408 B.C. Lindus, Ialysus, and Camirus founded the city of Rhodes on the NE tip of the island. The new city became the capital, replacing Lindus, and rapidly grew into a flourishing commercial, religious, and political center, thanks to its location and its wide commerce throughout the Mediterranean. The city later came under the influence of Sparta, from which it freed itself in 394 B.C. In 378 it entered the second Athenian Confederacy, from which it withdrew in 356 B.C. After the death of Alexander the Great, who had imposed a garrison on Rhodes as an ally of Persia against the Macedonians, the Rhodians allied themselves to Egypt and successfully withstood a year's siege by the Macedonians. Following this success, Rhodes entered into relations with Rome, and it was in this period that it reached the height of its importance and influence. Its commerce was carried on throughout the Mediter-

(obscured) errạnt, ardẹnt, actǫr; ch, chip; g, go; th, thin; ŧн, then; y, you;
(variable) ḍ as d or j, ṣ as s or sh, ṭ as t or ch, ẓ as z or zh.

ranean world. The code of maritime law developed by Rhodes was so good that 300 years later the Emperor Augustus adopted it for his entire empire. The city became an outstanding artistic and literary center. Lysippus the sculptor made his famous *Chariot of the Sun* there, and a distinctive Rhodian school of sculp-

Crouching Aphrodite, end of 2nd century B.C.
Archaeological Museum, Rhodes
Greek National Tourist Office

ture developed that numbered among its members Chares of Lindus, who made the famous *Colossus of Rhodes;* Philiscus, author of a group of the Muses; Apollonius and Tauriscus of Tralles, who executed the famous statue of the Dirce group, the so-called *Farnese Bull;* and Athenodorus, Polydorus, and Agesander, creators of the massive *Laocoön* group. Aeschines, the Athenian exile, founded a school of rhetoric at Rhodes that was later attended by Cato, Cicero, Caesar, Brutus, and other Romans. Splendid examples of Mycenaean pottery, dating from the 10th century B.C. and earlier have been found at Rhodes, and a distinctive style of glazed vases decorated with deer, the lotus

fat, fāte, fär, fȧll, ȧsk, fãre; net, mē, hėr; pin, pīne; not, nōte, mȯve, nôr; up, lūte, pu̇ll; oi, oil; ou out; (lightened) ẹlect, agǫny, ụnite;

flower, palm trees, and geometric designs, was in full flower by the 7th and 6th centuries B.C. The island was wholly sacred to Helius. Chariot-races, athletic and musical contests were held annually in the summer at the festival celebrated in his honor. Four horses were hurled into the sea each year at the festival as a sacrifice to him. About 278 B.C. the colossal bronze statue by Chares of Lindus was erected to Helius. This *Colossus,* one of the Seven Wonders of the ancient world, stood on the breakwater which protected the harbor of the city of Rhodes. It stood until 224 B.C., when it was hurled down by an earthquake; its fragments were melted down in 656 A.D. Augustus recognized Rhodes as a city allied to Rome. The emperor Vespasian incorporated it into the Roman Empire.

Rhoecus (rē′kus). Greek sculptor and architect; fl. c500 B.C. He was a native of Samos, where he built the famous temple of Hera, called by Herodotus one of the three greatest works of all Greece. Rhoecus was also supposed to have been the inventor of casting statues in bronze.

Rhyton (rī′ton). In ancient Greece, a type of drinking-vase, usually with one handle. In its usually curved form, pointed below, it corresponds to the primitive cup of horn. The lower part of the rhyton is generally molded into the form of a head of a man or, more often, of an animal, and is often pierced with a small hole through which the beverage was allowed to flow into the mouth.

S

Sacred Way. Ancient road in Greece from Athens to Eleusis, starting at the Dipylon Gate and traversing the Pass of Daphne. Over it passed every autumn from Athens the solemn procession for the celebration in the shrine of the great Eleusinian sanctuary of the mysteries in honor of Demeter, Persephone, and Iacchus. For almost its whole length it was bordered with tombs and chapels. At the beginning of the road, in the area known as Ceramicus, a number of the tombs remain in place, practically uninjured. Further along the modern road to Eleusis, whose line is almost identical with that of the Sacred Way, many architectural fragments are still visible, and some can be identified from the descriptions of Pausanias. At one point on the road is the monastery at Daphne which exhibits, in contrast with its Byzantine architecture, some remnants of French Gothic work. It was founded by the French dukes of Athens, and contains their tombs, but occupies the site of a temple to Apollo. Further on, toward the Bay of Salamis, there are considerable remains of a sanctuary to Aphrodite.

Samothrace (sam′ọ-thrās). [Also: *Khora, Samothrake, Samothraki.*] Wild, rocky island in the N part of the Aegean Sea, belonging to Greece, opposite the mouth of the Hebrus River and NW of the island of Imbrus. The island was famed in ancient times as the center of highly revered mysteries, those of the Cabiri, concerning which little is known. The rocky and difficult coast of the island, and the lack of anchorages, protected it from invasion, rendered it politically unimportant, and conserved the ancient mysteries intact. These mysteries assumed great importance under the Hellenistic rulers, and came to rival those of Eleusis in importance. It was when he went to Samothrace to be initiated into the mysteries that Philip II met Olympias, who became his wife and the mother of Alexander the Great. Arsinoë Philadelphus, the daughter of Ptolemy I who married her brother Ptolemy II, was banished to

VICTORY OF SAMOTHRACE, C190 B.C.
Louvre, Paris
Cultural Services of the French Embassy

Samothrace and became patroness of the sanctuary. She subsequently escaped and married Ptolemy II, but continued her benefactions to Samothrace. She and

Ptolemy dedicated the most important buildings on
the island. Perseus, last king of Macedonia, fled to
Samothrace after his defeat by Aemilius Paulus (168
B.C.) and sought refuge in the sanctuary; he was captured there and taken prisoner. At Samothrace a
French expedition found (1863) the famous statue
called the *Victory of Samothrace,* now in the Louvre.
Among the remains discovered on the island are the
ruins of a temple dating from the 6th century B.C.,
ruins of a later temple, probably that dedicated by
Ptolemy II, and a few rows of seats of an ancient theater. A New York University expedition directed by Karl
Lehmann has, in a number of excavation campaigns
since 1939, exposed the central area of the sanctuary.
The area of the island is about 71 square miles; its
highest point, 5248 feet.

Sarcophagus (sär-kof'a̱-gus). Typically, a coffin consisting of a rectangular box of stone with a heavy stone
cover, often decorated. The word means "flesh-eat-
ing," and is also applied to a kind of limestone so
active that it consumed the products of decomposition,
which suggests that this limestone was once the
material of choice for coffins of this type. The term has
since come to be applied to coffins of marble, por-
phyry, and other stones, terra-cotta, lead, wood, and
other materials; it is properly used only for coffins in
which the whole corpse was buried, not for smaller
chests in which the ashes of cremated bodies were
deposited. The most famous with classical connota-
tions are the Haghia Triadha sarcophagus, of terra-
cotta, with scenes of ritual painted in polychrome,
dating from the Cretan bronze age, and the famous
collection found at Sidon in Phoenicia, which includes
the splendid Alexander Sarcophagus and the Sarcophagus of the Mourning Women. In Hellenistic and
Roman times sarcophagi sculptured with scenes from
mythology, some executed with exquisite taste and
skill, became popular among the well-to-do, and led to

fat, fāte, fär, fȧll, ȧsk, fâre; net, mē, hêr; pin, pīne; not, nōte, mȯve,
nôr; up, lūte, pu̇ll; oi, oil; ou out; (lightened) e̱lect, ago̱ny, ūnite;

important developments in Early Christian art. Stone sarcophagi are readily adapted for re-use as baths, baptismal fonts, watering-troughs, dye vats, etc., and have been widely perverted to such purposes wherever found. (JJ)

Scopas (skō'pạs). Greek sculptor and architect; born in the island of Paros; fl. 4th century B.C. His first important work was the temple of Athena Alea at Tegea, built on the site of an older temple. The sculptures of it included scenes of the Calydonian Boar Hunt and the battle between Achilles and Telephus. Battered fragments of these sculptures remain. Scopas probably went to Athens c377 B.C., and remained there 25 years, when he went to Halicarnassus to superintend the sculpture of the Mausoleum. The fragments from this monument in the British Museum probably give us our most reliable information as to Scopas' style; but he is generally conceded to have led, or to have typified, a departure from the earlier serene, reposeful treatment of sculpture to the expression of strong emotion in facial expressions and in the movements of the figures. A doubtful passage of Pausanias suggests that he is represented in the sculpture recovered from the Artemisium at Ephesus. The *Apollo Citharoedus* of the Vatican has been associated with Scopas as a copy of his statue. The original of one Niobe group was by either Scopas or Praxiteles, probably Scopas.

Scyllis (sil'is). Greek sculptor of the archaic period, active c580 B.C., and said to have invented the art of carving in marble. See entry under *Dipoenus* and *Scyllis.*

Skyphos (skī'fos). In ancient Greece, a large drinking-cup shaped like the kylix, and, like it, with two handles not extending above the rim, but without a foot.

Smilis (smī'lis). Aeginetan sculptor, c580–540 B.C. Some say he was a contemporary of Daedalus. Among his works were the images of the Horae (Seasons) in the temple of Hera at Olympia, and an image of Hera in her temple at Samos.

SCOPAS
Battle of Greeks and Amazons, from the E frieze of the Mausoleum at Halicarnassus
British Museum

Sophilus (sof'i-lus). Athenian potter and vase-painter in the black-figure style, active at the end of the 7th and the beginning of the 6th century B.C. His signature has been preserved on the fragments of three vases. A fragment from a large mixing bowl (Athens), signed "Sophilus made me," shows a chariot race on the shoulder, and is inscribed "Patroclus' funeral games," a rare instance of a vase-painter giving a title to his painting. Spectators watching the race sit in a grandstand. Beside one of the spectators the name Achilles is inscribed.

Sosias (sō'si-as). Attic potter, active at the beginning of the 5th century B.C. The painter who decorated his work, in the red-figure style, is known as the Sosias Painter. Of two works definitely attributed to him, a kylix (Berlin) shows Achilles binding up the wounds of Patroclus and is admired for the subject and the concentrated rendering thereof.

Stamnos (stam'nos). In ancient Greece, a large water- or wine-vase closely resembling the hydria, but generally with a shorter neck, and provided merely with the two small handles on the sides of the paunch, the larger handle behind being absent.

Stereobate (stèr'e-ō-bāt). In architecture, the substructure, foundation, or solid platform upon which a building is erected. In columnar buildings it includes the stylobate, which is the uppermost step or platform of the foundation upon which the columns stand.

Stoa (stō'a). A *porticus* or colonnade, a very important type of public building in ancient Greece and Italy. The term means "row of columns." In its simplest form the stoa was a long, narrow, one-story structure, its roof supported on the side facing the street, marketplace, or temple enclosure by columns, on the other side by a blank wall, with ends open or closed. The plan was elaborated in various ways: with a second row of columns, with a second story, with projecting bays at each end, with two wings (forming an L), with three wings (forming three sides of a square or rectangle, the open side regularly toward the south to take the fullest advantage of winter sun and summer shade), with four wings, with a row of shops behind the columns, and so on. In the Athenian Agora one stoa has a wall on the longitudinal axis and columns on either long side, in effect, two stoas back-to-back. In Rome one porticus has no solid wall, the roof being supported solely by columns. At Delos the term stoa is applied to a large enclosed rectangular building, the Hypostyle Hall. Less sturdy in construction than temples, stoas were particularly vulnerable to earthquake, fire and the crowbars of vandals, and no stoa or porticus has survived intact; the Stoa of Attalus, at Athens, restored as the Agora Museum by the American excavators of the Agora, demonstrates better than any other the usefulness and adaptability of this popular and widespread building type. Stoas in Greece, and porticus in Rome, were places where lawyers and businessmen met their clients, magistrates conferred, teachers lectured, idlers lounged, and citizens generally took refuge from rain and sun. In the lexicon of philosophy, *The Stoa* refers to the Stoa Poikile or Painted Colonnade, bordering the Athenian Agora, where Zeno the Stoic and his successors lectured. (JJ)

Stylobate (stī′lọ̄-bāt). In architecture, a continuous basement upon which columns are placed to raise them above the level of the ground or a floor; particularly, the uppermost step of the stereobate of a columnar building, upon which rests an entire range of columns. It is distinguished from a pedestal, which, when it occurs in this use, supports only a single column.

Sunium (sö′ni-um) or *Sunium Promontorium* (prom-ọn-tō′ri-um). [Also: *Sounion, Cape Colonna.*] In ancient geography, a lofty headland running into the sea at the SE extremity of Attica. At the summit, enclosed by a fortification wall and approached through propylaea or formal entrance gates, are the striking ruins of a splendid Periclean Doric hexastyle temple of the sea-god Poseidon, designed by the *Theseum Architect*, constructed c444 B.C. to replace an earlier temple, and conspicuous far out to sea. It is built of a local marble

Temple of Poseidon, c444 B.C.
Greek Embassy Press and Information Service

which unlike Pentelic marble has not weathered to a russet patina, but retains its dazzling whiteness. The view of the Aegean and its islands from the temple terrace is superb. Outside the sanctuary, at a little distance, are the foundations of an Ionic temple of Athena, unusual in that it had exterior columns on the front (E) and one flank (S) only. According to Homer, Phrontis, pilot of Menelaus, was struck down by the arrows of Apollo as his ship rounded Sunium on the return from Troy. (JJ)

T

Tanagra (tan′a̤-gra̤, ta̤-nag′ra̤). In ancient geography, a town of Boeotia, Greece, situated near the Asopus River, about 24 miles NW of Athens. The inhabitants in ancient times claimed descent from Apollo and Poseidon, and said their town was named for Tanagra, a daughter of Aeolus or, as some say, of the river-god Asopus. Among the temples of Tanagra in antiquity were those of Themis, Apollo, Aphrodite, Hermes, and Dionysus. In the last was a marble image of the god by the sculptor Calamis. There was also an image of a headless Triton. According to legend, a Triton attacked the women of Tanagra when they went to bathe in the sea to purify themselves before celebrating the rites of Dionysus. The women called on the god to protect them; he came and killed the Triton after a great struggle. But others say the Triton used to come from the sea and attack the cattle of the Tanagraeans. To catch him, a bowl of wine was set on the beach. The Triton drank of it and fell into a drunken slumber on the sand, whereupon a man of Tanagra cut off his head. Some say the tomb of Orion was at Tanagra. The tomb of the lyric poetess Corinna was also there, with a painting depicting her binding her hair with the victor's crown after a contest with Pindar. A victory was gained here in 457 B.C. by the Spartans over the Athenians and their allies. Its extensive necropolis has made this obscure town famous, for from it came (c1874) the first of the charming Tanagra figurines of terra-cotta which drew attention to the antiquities of this type. Such figurines, previously ignored, have since been eagerly sought and found in great quantities not only at Tanagra but upon a great number of sites in all parts of the Greek world.

fat, fāte, fär, fâll, a̤sk, fāre; net, mē, hėr; pin, pīne; not, nōte, möve, nôr; up, lūte, pu̇ll; oi, oil; ou out; (lightened) e̤lect, agǫny, ūnite;

Telesterion (te-les-ter′i-ǫn). A hall of initiation (*telesthenai* "to be initiated"), where the rites and ceremonies of admission to membership in the mystery religions were performed; especially, that at Eleusis near Athens. The Telesterion at Eleusis, at first a shrine of modest dimensions, was several times rebuilt on a larger scale. In its final 5th-century B.C. form it was a large building, square in plan, enclosing an area of about 29,000 square feet, with a Doric portico of 12 columns, and six entrances. The roof was supported by seven rows of six columns, like the hypostyle halls of Egypt, and along the four walls were eight rows of narrow stone seats. A religious drama or pageant based on the myth of Demeter was performed in this hall for the candidates for initiation. The initiates were forbidden to reveal the details of the ceremony, and the secret was kept so well that modern scholarship has not penetrated it. However, there are hints that the ceremony told of the rape by Hades of Demeter's daughter Persephone, Demeter's search, her kindly reception at Eleusis, and her gift of agriculture. (JJ)

Temenos (tem′ę-nos). In Greek antiquity, a sacred enclosure or precinct; a piece of land marked off from common uses and dedicated to a god; a precinct, usually surrounded by a barrier, allotted to a temple or sanctuary, or consecrated for any reason.

Tetrastyle (tet′rạ-stīl). In classical architecture, a term applied to a portico with four columns on the front or to a roof or ceiling supported by four columns.

Thera (thir′ạ, thē′rạ). [Also: ***Thira, Santorini.***] Volcanic island in the S part of the Cyclades. At an early date, about 1500 B.C. according to some scholars, a catastrophic series of eruptions caused part of the island, including most of the volcano, to sink into the sea. In 1967, near Akrotiri (q.v.), in the south of Thera, a team of archaeologists discovered and began excavating the site of a Minoan city abandoned as a result of the 1500 B.C. (?) eruptions. Its streets and houses have been preserved by the layer of volcanic ash 100 to 300 feet thick that covers most of the island. Its ancient name as yet unknown, this outpost of Minoan civilization has yielded many valuable finds. Objects discovered range from remnants of food and medicines still in their containers, household utensils, and furniture outlined in the ash, to pottery of relatively sophisticated design and a group of remarkable frescoes. "The Room of the Lilies," one of these frescoes, is the largest nearly intact fresco of that period ever found in Greece. The

ROOM OF THE LILIES
Detail, Two Swallows and a Lily, fresco found at Akrotiri, Thera
National Museum, Athens
T.A.P. Service

city may originally have extended about one mile in length and possibly held 20,000 to 30,000 inhabitants. *Thersilion* (thėr-sil′i-ọn). The convention hall of the federal assembly of the Arcadian League at Megalopolis, named for its founder, built in the 4th century B.C., and notable for its size (over 35,000 square feet), and the ingenious arrangement of the interior columns supporting the roof, which, in order to reduce to the minimum their obstruction of the view from any part of the hall, are ranged in lines radiating from the speaker's platform. The Thersilion is connected to the theater of Megalopolis, with which it forms an architectural whole; its Doric entrance portico of 14 columns faced the auditorium and served as a permanent scene. Megalopolis was destroyed in 222 B.C. and the Thersilion apparently was not rebuilt. (JJ)

Theseum (thē-sē'um). A hieron or sanctuary near the Agora of Athens, dedicated to the hero-king Theseus, but not yet identified by the Agora excavators. Here were reburied, as those of Theseus, the bones brought by Cimon from Scyrus; on its walls were famous paintings, and it was a familiar place of refuge. The well-preserved Periclean marble temple which stands on the terrace dominating the Agora on the west was formerly considered to be a temple of Theseus, and is

Theseum, c450–440 B.C.
Greek National Tourist Office

(obscured) errant, ardent, actor; ch, chip; g, go; th, thin; ᵺ, then; y, you;
(variable) ḍ as d or j, ṣ as s or sh, ṭ as t or ch, ẓ as z or zh.

pictured under the name of Theseum in many older works on the antiquities of Athens. It has now been shown beyond reasonable doubt that this temple was dedicated to Hephaestus, or to Hephaestus and Athena, and it is probable that the real sanctuary of Theseus did not contain a temple. In the meantime, however, the erroneous identification had suggested a name, the "Theseum Architect," for the otherwise nameless architect who designed the temple of Hephaestus and other structures, and this designation continues in use. (JJ)

Theseum Architect. A name, inspired by the erroneous identification of the Theseum at Athens with the temple of Hephaestus, retained as a convenient designation for the otherwise nameless master architect who designed the Periclean marble temples of Hephaestus and Ares at Athens, of Poseidon at Sunium, and of Nemesis at Rhamnus. (JJ)

Thymele (thim'ȩ̄-lē). In Greek antiquity, an altar; particularly, the small altar of Dionysus which occupied the central point of the orchestra of the Greek theater, and was a visible token of the religious character of the dramatic representations. Literally, "a place for sacrifice."

Timanthes (ti-man'thēz). Greek painter of Sicyon; born in the island of Cythnus in the Cyclades; fl. c400 B.C. He is known mainly as the painter of one of the great pictures of antiquity, the *Sacrifice of Iphigenia,* in which Agamemnon conceals his uncontrollable grief by covering his head with his mantle. This picture was a favorite of Cicero. Pliny's remark that there is "always something more implied than expressed in his work" is suggestive of bold and generalized execution.

Timomachus (ti-mom'a̧-kus). Painter, of Byzantium, fl. in the 1st century B.C. According to Pliny, Julius Caesar paid a large sum for two of his pictures, an *Ajax* and a *Medea.* The *Medea* of Timomachus was not less praised in song and epigram than the *Aphrodite* of Apelles (an echo of the original may perhaps be seen in some of the Pompeian wall paintings). His *Iphigenia in Tauris* and a *Gorgon* were also celebrated.

Timotheus (tĭ-mō′thē̯-us, -moth′ē̯-us; tī-). Greek sculptor, probably from Epidaurus; fl. 4th century B.C. He is best known as the oldest of the four sculptors (the others being Scopas, Leochares, and Bryaxis) who created the Mausoleum, the tomb of Mausolus, satrap of Caria, at Halicarnassus, which was completed c333 B.C. The relief panel of the Amazon frieze from the southern face is attributed to Timotheus. It is thought that he also contributed sculptural ornamentation to the Temple of Asclepius at Epidaurus.

Tiryns (tī′rinz). In ancient geography, a city in Argolis, Greece, situated near the coast SE of Argos, and about three miles N of Nauplia. According to tradition, the region was first occupied by Pelasgians, who fell under the domination of Danaus when he came to Argolis from Egypt with his 50 daughters. Following internecine wars, the kingdom of Danaus was divided among his descendants. Acrisius became ruler of the region of Argos and his brother Proetus became king of the area about Tiryns and founded the city. According to legend, he imported Cyclopes from Lycia to build its "Cyclopean" walls of enormous, irregular stones. It fell under the domination of Mycenae but with the Dorian invasion of the Peloponnesus recovered its independence. In the Persian Wars Tiryns sent 200 men to the Battle of Plataea (479 B.C.). Their names were inscribed on the tripods dedicated at Delphi in celebration of the Greek victory. In 468 B.C. Argos, jealous of the honor paid Tiryns for its part in the Persian Wars, in which Argos had played no heroic part, conquered Tiryns and destroyed the city.

The city was built on a low rocky hill that rose above the plain of Argos. The ancient city, occupying the hill and the area of the plain at its base, was older than Mycenae, and dates from the 3rd millennium B.C. After

TIMOTHEUS
Battle of Greeks and Amazons, from the S frieze of the Mausoleum at Halicarnassus
British Museum

fat, fāte, fär, fåll, åsk, fāre; net, mē, hėr; pin, pīne; not, nōte, möve, nôr; up, lūte, půll; oi, oil; ou out; (lightened) ĕlect, agǫny, ūnite;

2000 B.C. the citadel on the summit of the low rock was enclosed by walls, within which remains of a pre-Mycenaean palace have been found. Tiryns is celebrated for its antiquities, including Cyclopean walls, gates, and the palace (excavated by Heinrich Schliemann and Wilhelm Dörpfeld, 1884–85). The citadel is a famous memorial of early Greek civilization. The massive walls, built of great blocks, some of which weigh as much as 13 tons, with the interstices filled with small stones, surround the summit of an oblong hill. In the *Iliad* Homer speaks of Tiryns as "mighty of ramparts." Pausanias, who visited it in the 2nd century A.D., said it was unnecessary to go to Egypt to see the pyramids when there were such wonders as Tiryns at home. The acropolis at Tiryns is divided into three terraces, of which the highest was occupied by the palace and royal quarters, and included the well-known galleries of arcades resembling pointed arches. These galleries gave on to chambers constructed in the thickness of the walls and were unique in Greek architecture. They were used as storage areas in time of peace and as armories and places of shelter in time of war. The middle terrace, north and west of the royal quarters, reinforced the acropolis and was occupied by those connected with the royal household. To the north, and separated by a wall, was the lower terrace where the garrison was quartered, and to which the population of the city at the base of the hill withdrew in times of invasion. As at Mycenae, the principal approach to the acropolis was by a passageway made of enormous blocks of stone, more carefully dressed and fitted than the surrounding walls, and was so placed that the right, or unshielded, side of an approaching enemy was exposed to the defenders in the citadel. Within the walls of the acropolis there are remains of an extensive prehistoric palace, with outer and inner courts, men's apartments, bathroom, and secluded women's quarters, the whole corresponding with the

(obscured) errᶏnt, ardᶒnt, actǫr; ch, chip; g, go; th, thin; ᴛʜ, then; y, you;
(variable) ḍ as d or j, ṣ as s or sh, ṭ as t or ch, ẓ as z or zh.

spirit of the Homeric picture. The floor plan of the palace is still plainly visible. A cistern and remains of a drainage system have been found at Tiryns, as well as a royal altar surrounded by a ditch into which the blood of sacrificial victims flowed. Wall paintings and other details of high interest were found by Schliemann.

Tleson (tlē'son). Attic potter of the 6th century B.C., who specialized in small cups. A group of these cups is known as the Little Master cups from the exquisite miniature paintings on them. The decorator of Tleson's cups worked in the black-figure style and is known as the Tleson Painter. A cup (British Museum) from the third quarter of the 6th century B.C. shows an almost prancing hunter, accompanied by his dog, carrying small animals on a pole slung over his shoulder. It is signed, "Tleson, son of Nearchus, made." Another cup (Metropolitan Museum, N.Y.), c540 B.C., has the same inscription.

Torso Belvedere (tôr'sō bel-vẹ-dir'). Ancient figure of Heracles signed by the Athenian sculptor Apollonius, now in the Vatican, Rome. It is ascribed to the middle of the 1st century B.C., and is remarkable for the anatomical knowledge evidenced by the sitting position of the figure.

Tower of the Winds. Horologium or water clock erected by the Syrian Andronicus Cyrrhestes at Athens in the 1st century B.C. It is octagonal in plan, 26 feet in diameter, and 42 feet high. Toward the top of each face is sculptured a figure representing one of the eight principal winds, with appropriate attributes. The structure was surmounted by a bronze Triton which served as a weathervane.

Triglyph (trī'glif). In architecture, a structural member in the frieze of the Doric order, repeated at equal intervals, usually over every column and over the middle of every intercolumniation. The typical Greek triglyph is a massive block incised with two entire vertical grooves cut to a right angle, called *glyphs,* framed between three fillets, and with a semi-groove at each side. The block is grooved on both sides to receive the adjoining metopes, which are thin slabs slid into their places from above. The triglyphs represent the ends of the ceiling-beams of the primitive wooden construction.

Tripod (trī'pod). In pre-classical and classical antiquity, a seat, table, or other article resting on three feet. Specifically 1) A three-legged seat or table. 2) A pot or caldron used for heating water or boiling meat, and either raised upon a three-legged frame or stand, or made with three feet in the same piece with itself. 3) A bronze altar, originally identical in form with the caldron described above. It had three rings at the top to serve as handles, and in many representations shows a central support or upright in addition to the three legs. It was when seated upon a tripod of this nature, over a cleft in the ground in the innermost sanctuary, that the Pythian priestesses at Delphi gave their oracular responses. The celebrity of this tripod, which was especially sacred to the Pythian Apollo and was a usual attribute of him, led to innumerable imitations of it, which were made to be used in sacrifice, and ornamented tripods of similar form, sometimes made of the precious metals, were given as prizes at The Pythian Games and elsewhere, and were frequently placed as votive gifts in temples, especially in those of Apollo.

Troy (troi). [Also: *Ilium;* Latin, *Troia, Troja.*] Ancient city in Asia Minor, famous in Greek legend as the capital of Priam and the object of the siege by the allied Greeks under Agamemnon. According to legend, the city was founded by Teucer, an immigrant from Crete who was the son of the Cretan river Scamander and the nymph Idaea. From him the people were called Teucrians. In the reign of Teucer, Dardanus came to his kingdom from Samothrace. Teucer gave him land in the region and his daughter Batia in marriage. Dardanus built a city at the foot of Mount Ida which he called Dardania. Tros, the grandson of Dardanus, called his people Trojans and named the city Troy. One son of Tros was Ilus, the father of Laomedon and the grandfather of Priam. Another was Assaracus, the ancestor of Aeneas. And a third son was Ganymede, carried off to Olympus by Zeus. Ilion, the city that Ilus founded in obedience to an oracle, was joined with Dardania and Troy and the whole came to be called Troy or Ilium. The location of Troy near the Hellespont and the entrance to the Propontis and the Euxine Sea, gave it command of trade from the Aegean islands and Greece to the region about the Euxine Sea. It was the strongest power on the coast of Asia Minor. The Trojan War, celebrated in the *Iliad* of Homer, is now thought to have been waged to destroy this control and to secure access to the lands about the Euxine Sea. According to Homer, the war lasted ten years. The first nine were occupied in raids on the cities of the Troad which supplied and supported Troy, for Priam's rule extended from the island of Lesbos to the Hellespont to Phrygia. In the tenth year the city itself was attacked and finally fell. The date for its fall is c1200 B.C.

The site of this Homeric city was generally believed in antiquity to be identical with that of the Greek Ilium (the modern Hissarlik); and this view has been supported in later times, most notably by Heinrich Schliemann, who followed the descriptions in the *Iliad* literally and whose explorations (1871 *et seq.*) at Hissarlik laid bare remains of a series of ancient towns, one above the other. The third and later the second from the bottom he identified with the Homeric town, those levels showing the effects of a conflagration and massive ruins. On the other hand, some scholars regarded the situation of Ilium as irreconcilable with Homer's description of Troy, and preferred a site in the neighborhood of the later Bunarbashi, holding Schliemann's results to be inconclusive. More recent investigations indicate, however, that Schliemann was

fat, fāte, fär, fåll, àsk, fāre; net, mē, hèr; pin, pīne; not, nōte, möve, nôr; up, lūte, pùll; oi, oil; ou out; (lightened) ẹlect, agǫny, ụnite;

correct about the site, but that the sixth, or more probably, the seventh level was ancient Ilium. Schliemann's and subsequent excavations on the site have revealed that a city existed there as early as the 3rd millennium B.C. Priam's city, erected on the ruins of earlier cities, was on a mound commanding the plains of the Scamander River and its tributary the Simois. It was larger than the earlier cities and was surrounded by a massive wall, built in the reign of Laomedon, according to legend, by Apollo and Poseidon with the aid of Aeacus. The wall was pierced by gates, of which the Scaean Gate is mentioned in the *Iliad.* On the highest point within the walls rose the palace-fortress. On the lower slopes were the houses of the inhabitants of the city, remains of which have been found. Gold ornaments and pottery indicate that the city was of the level of the Mycenaean civilization. The city of Troy remained a center of interest throughout antiquity for its historic and legendary significance. Xerxes stopped there on his way to invade Greece (481 B.C.) and offered sacrifices at the shrine of Ilian Athena to the shades of the ancient heroes of the Trojan War. Alexander the Great stopped there, 334 B.C., and saw the arms the heroes of the Trojan War had carried, including the shield of Achilles. The Romans, claiming descent from Trojan Aeneas, honored it. Lucius Scipio offered sacrifice to Ilian Athena. Sulla rebuilt the city after it had been destroyed by his opponent, the Roman general Fimbria. Augustus honored the city and enlarged its territory. After the 4th century A.D. the city fell into ruins, its site was abandoned, and even the location of the historic city was forgotten and lost until Schliemann's discovery of it.

(obscured) errạnt, ardẹnt, actọr; ch, chip; g, go; th, thin; ŦH, then; y, you; (variable) ḍ as d or j, ṣ as s or sh, ṭ as t or ch, ẓ as z or zh.

——— V ———

Vase-painting. From the variety and domesticity of the subjects treated, Greek vase-painting is of the greatest importance for the light shed by it upon every phase of ancient life; and from the art side it is equally valuable, not only from the fine decorative and creative quality which it frequently shows, but from the information that it supplies regarding the great art of Greek wall and easel painting, which has almost entirely perished. Painted ware in Crete in the Early Minoan Period (2800–2000 B.C.; a date for the beginning of the period somewhat later than that suggested by Sir Arthur Evans) consisted of simple designs—bands, wavy lines, plumes, curvilinear patterns—in dark paint on light and light paint on dark backgrounds, using black, varying shades of red, and white. Middle Minoan (2000–1550 B.C.) ware adds naturalistic lily and other plant patterns. In the Late Minoan Period (1550–1100 B.C.), designs inspired by marine life, as befitted a sea power, are widely employed. Octopuses, dolphins, fish, shells, and marine growths, first naturalistic and later stylized, with the occasional admission of the human figure, are skillfully accommodated to the shapes and surfaces that they decorate. On the Greek mainland a parallel development occurred in the Mycenaean Age (c1600–1100 B.C.), so called from its center about Mycenae. Following the Dorian invasion (c1100 B.C.), a geometric style of decoration replaces the patterns of the Minoan-Mycenaean Period. Formal arrangements, in bands or zones, of parallel lines, zigzags, swastikas, maeanders or variations of the key design, and checkerboards completely cover the vase, and give to this period the name Geometric. Later in the period (9th and 8th centuries B.C.) the Attic pot-

ters, particularly, produced huge amphorae, some as
much as five feet high, which in addition to the geometric zones sometimes carry a scenic frieze. Slim,
angular human figures, drawn schematically in silhouette, appear in the friezes, the designs becoming
freer with the advance of time. Called Dipylon vases
because many of them were found in the cemeteries
outside the Dipylon Gate of Athens, and often used as
monuments on graves, many of these show some part
of the funeral ritual or procession in the frieze inserted
between zones of geometric patterns. In the 8th and
7th centuries, increased trade activity with the cities of
Ionia and beyond led to the introduction of Oriental
motifs in vase decoration—palmettes, lotuses, rosettes, friezes of fabulous monsters, spirals. Geometric
patterns gradually disappear as the space reserved for
a pictorial panel increases. On the mainland of Greece,
Corinth was the most important center for the production of vases in the Ionic style. The characteristic feature of the Corinthian style is the superposition of
bands of animals and monsters, with rosettes and
elaborate flowered and fringed borders, the whole following very closely the Assyrian and Phrygian metal-
work and embroideries, which were abundantly
imported into Greece at this time. Proto-Corinthian
vases (725–640 B.C.) progressed from a highly developed geometric style on small vessels, through a stage
where friezes of monsters and animals predominated,
to a late phase in which the decoration consists of
finely executed miniature paintings, generally of mythological subjects. The class of vessels, larger on the
whole, called Corinthian (c640–550 B.C.), continued
the use of friezes of animals and then developed, in the
7th century, the technique known as the black-figure
style. This style, perfected at Corinth and adopted by
Athenian potters, shows little Oriental influence; it is
thoroughly Hellenic. In black-figure the decoration is
painted in black silhouette directly on the clay. Details

(obscured) errȧnt, ardȩnt, actǫr; ch, chip; g, go; th, thin; ꞄH, then; y, you;
(variable) ḍ as d or j, ş as s or sh, ṭ as t or ch, ẓ as z or zh.

within the silhouette are incised with a graver. Occasionally red, purple, or white are sparingly used for decorative accent. The subjects of the masters of the black-figure style are most often from mythology; Heracles, for example, with the great variety of his adventures, is a favorite subject; Theseus and Perseus are also popular. Scenes from daily life begin to appear. The drawing is strong and archaic; the effect is decorative. The heads of the human figures are in profile, but the eye is full face. Men's eyes are round, women's are almond-shaped. The flesh of women is white. Bodies are in profile or with the shoulders and chest front view, the hips and legs in profile. Among the masters of the black-figure technique are Timonidas of Corinth (early 6th century B.C.); his contemporary, Sophilus of Athens (q.v.); Nearchus (q.v.), painter and potter; Exekias (q.v.), painter and potter; Cleitias (q.v.), painter who worked with the potter Ergotimus; the Amasis Painter (q.v.); and the Tleson Painter (q.v.).

By the middle of the 6th century B.C., Athens eclipsed Corinth as the center of the production of painted vases. A new technique developed there, the red-figure style, in which the background is painted black and the reddish color of the vessel itself is reserved for the figures. Details of the figures are drawn in black or a diluted black. The advantage of this technique is that it liberates the artist from the engraver, the brush giving greater fluidity than the graving tool. The black ground also heightens and sets off the red figures. At the same time, it intensifies the design effect. The black-figure and red-figure style existed side by side for many years. Indeed some masters, as Epictetus (q.v.) and the Andocides Painter (q.v.), worked in both, and on occasion used both on the same vessel, black-figure on one side and red-figure on the other. Toward the end of the first quarter of the 5th century B.C., however, the red-figure superseded the black-figure, except in the decoration of Pana-

fat, fāte, fär, fâll, ȧsk, fãre; net, mē, hėr; pin, pīne; not, nōte, mȯve, nôr; up, lūte, pu̇ll; oi, oil; ou out; (lightened) ēlect, agǫny, ūnite;

thenaic amphorae, which, by tradition, continued to be painted in black-figure and in a traditional archaic manner. Subjects of the red-figure artists are at first from mythology, then increasingly from daily life, as, the potter's shop, the shoemaker's shop, the music lesson, feasting and dancing, etc. Over 500 artists of the red-figure style have been identified, not, however, by their own names. Their identities are variously indicated, sometimes from the potter who is known to have thrown their vessels, as the Cleophrades Painter (q.v.), the Brygos Painter (q.v.), Pistoxenus Painter, Sosias Painter (q.v.), Sotades Painter; sometimes from a distinctive subject of their paintings, as the Penthesilea Painter, Pan Painter, Niobid Painter, Achilles Painter; sometimes from the location of an example of their work, as the Berlin Painter, Chicago Painter, Providence Painter. Among those whose names are known are: Euthymides (q.v.), Euphronius (q.v.), Onesimus (q.v.), Duris (q.v.), Phintias (q.v.), Oltos (q.v.), Myson (q.v.), and Macron (q.v.).

Another technique, employed generally only for the interiors of kylixes and for the decoration of lecythi, covered the natural clay with a white or creamy slip, and used this as a surface for painting outline figures in various colors. Greek vase-painting reached its height in the 5th century B.C. Attic ware was distributed throughout the Mediterranean region. Many of the surviving examples were found outside the borders of the Greek mainland. After the 5th century the quality of painted vases declined, but the art survived until the 3rd century, when painted pottery was no longer produced.

Venus de Milo (mī'lō). [Also: ***Venus of Melos.***] Greek statue in the Louvre, Paris, perhaps the most admired single existing work of antiquity. It was found in 1829 on the island of Melos, and in date appears to fall between the time of Phidias and that of Praxiteles, or c400 B.C. The statue represents a majestic woman, undraped to the hips, standing with the weight on the right foot and with the head turned slightly toward the left. The arms are broken off, and there is a dispute as to their original position.

VENUS DE MILO, c400 B.C.
Louvre, Paris
Cultural Services of the French Embassy

Victory of Samothrace (sam'ọ̄-thrās). [Also: ***Winged Victory.***] One of the greatest art monuments of antiquity, found in Samothrace in 1863, and now in the Louvre,

fat, fāte, fär, fȧll, ȧsk, fãre; net, mē, hėr; pin, pīne; not, nōte, mȯve, nôr; up, lūte, pṳll; oi, oil; ou out; (lightened) ẹlect, agọny, ụnite;

Paris. The colossal winged figure (of which the head has been lost) stands, with full drapery blown by the wind, on the prow of a trireme. The work is of Hellenistic date.

Winged Victory. See *Victory of Samothrace.*
Wingless Victory, Temple of. See *Athena Nike, Temple of.*

Z

Zeuxis (zōk′sis). Greek painter; born at Heraclea, in Lucania; fl. at the close of the 5th century B.C. He formed his style at Athens under the influence of Apollodorus, worked at various other cities, and finally settled at Ephesus. He is said to have introduced light and shadow into his paintings to give mass. He was also especially successful in achieving illusion. The story is told of a contest between him and Parrhasius. Zeuxis painted grapes so lifelike that birds came and pecked at them. Parrhasius painted a filmy drapery that deceived Zeuxis. Among his principal works were *Zeus on His Throne Surrounded by Gods, Eros Crowned with Roses* (in the temple of Aphrodite at Athens), the *Marsyas* (in the temple of Concord at Rome), the *Centaur Family* (described by Lucian), the *Alcmene of the Argentines, Heracles as a Child,* the *Helena* (in the temple of Lucanïan Hera), and the *Boy with Grapes.*

(obscured) errạnt, ardẹnt, actǫr; ch, chip; g, go; th, thin; ᴛʜ, then; y, you; (variable) ḍ as d or j, ş as s or sh, ţ as t or ch, ẓ as z or zh.

709.38 N432c1
The New Century handbook of Gr

AAI-9882
060101 001

0 0003 0134242 4
Johnson State College

John Dewey Library
Johnson State College
Johnson, VT. 05656